Easy Cookie Recipes

Also by Addie Gundry

Everyday Dinner Ideas:
103 Easy Recipes for Chicken, Pasta, and
Other Dishes Everyone Will Love

No-Bake Desserts:
103 Easy Recipes for No-Bake Cookies, Bars, and Treats

Family Favorite Casserole Recipes:
103 Comforting Breakfast Casseroles, Dinner Ideas,
and Desserts Everyone Will Love

Easy Cookie Recipes

103 Best Recipes for Chocolate Chip Cookies,
Cake Mix Creations, Bars, and
Holiday Treats Everyone Will Love

Addie Gundry

St. Martin's Griffin 🦅 New York

Any product brand names listed as recipe ingredients or referred to in recipe titles are trademarks of their respective brand owners. This is an independent work not endorsed, sponsored, or authorized by those brand owners.

EASY COOKIE RECIPES. Text and photography copyright © 2017 by Prime Publishing LLC. All rights reserved. Printed in the United States of America. For information, address St. Martin's Press, 175 Fifth Avenue, New York, N.Y. 10010.

www.stmartins.com

Photographs by Megan Von Schönhoff

The Library of Congress Cataloging-in-Publication Data is available upon request.

ISBN 978-1-250-13880-4 (trade paperback)
ISBN 978-1-250-13881-1 (ebook)

Our books may be purchased in bulk for promotional, educational, or business use. Please contact your local bookseller or the Macmillan Corporate and Premium Sales Department at 1-800-221-7945, extension 5442, or by email at MacmillanSpecialMarkets@macmillan.com.

First Edition: November 2017

10 9 8 7 6 5 4 3 2 1

To gravitytank, Lucas, and Kyleigh.

Thank you for teaching me that good ideas come from
bad ones; that hacking, gluing, and mashing things together
is just as tasty as something from scratch; and for showing me
what it means to create in a collaborative culture.

Contents

Introduction   1

1
Bar Cookies

Apple Pie Bars   5

3-Layer Nanaimo Bars   6

Seven Layers of Heaven   9

Five-Layer Chocolate Cherry Bars   10

Peanut Butter Bars   13

Strawberry Cheesecake Bars   14

Peanut Butter Bacon Bars   17

No-Bake Coconut Graham Cracker
Cookie Bars   18

Zebra Bars   21

Peanut Butter Swirl Bars   22

Oatmeal Chocolate Raisin Bars   25

Stir and Bake Bars   26

Salted Caramel Bars   29

Trillionaire Dessert Bars   30

Dreamboat Caramel Bars   33

Chocolate Peanut Butter Bars   34

Texas Gold Bars   37

Raspberry Oatmeal Cookie Bars   38

Better-Than-Anything Scotcharoos   41

2
Cake Mix Cookies

Chocolate Cake Mix Cookies   45

Whipped Lemon Cookies   46

10-Minute Miracle Cookies   49

Easy Oatmeal Cookies   50

Lemon Pie Bars   53

Gooey Magic Cake Bars   54

Chocolate Chip Bars   57

M&M's Drop Cookies   58

Cake Mix Magic Cream Cheese Squares   61

10-Minute Cool Whip Cookies   62

Funfetti Cake Batter Cookies   65

3
Fruits and Nuts

No-Bake Cookie Clusters   69

Orange Cream Bars   70

Pecan Sandies   73

Strawberry Bars   74

2-Ingredient Lemon Bars   77

Chocolate Cherry Blossom Cookies   78

No-Bake Almond Coconut Cookies   81

Lemon Coconut Cookies   82

Tropical Paradise Cookies   85

Cream Cheese Strawberry Cookies   86

Crazy Good Cranberry Orange Cookies   89

Banana Bread Bites   90

Butter Pecan Cake Mix Squares   93

Blueberry Muffin Cookies   94

4
Sugar and Spice

Home-Style Amish Sugar Cookies   99

Bite-Size Cinnamon Roll Cookies   100

Spice Bars   103

Buttery Sugar Cookies   104

Snickerdoodles   107

Ginger Snaps   108

Soda Pop Cookies   111

Danish Spice Cookies   112

Linzer Cookies   115

Maple Sugar Cookies   116

Salted Caramel Bites   119

Buttery Thumbprints   120

Grandma's Spice Cookies   123

5
Chocolate

The Best Chocolate Chip Cookies Ever   127

Alex's Cowboy Cookies   128

Chocolate Haystacks   131

Chewy Brownie Cookies   132

Gooey Turtle Bars   135

Incredible Buckeye Brownie Cookies   136

5-Minute No-Bake Cookies   139

Cream Cheese Chocolate Chip Cookies   140

Monster Cookies   143

Mint Chocolate Cookies   144

Chocolate Shortbread   147

Toasted S'mores Cookies   148

My-Goodness-These-Are-Amazing Cookies   151

Mocha Polka Dot Cookies   152

Chocolate Chip Cookies 'n' Cream   155

Caramel Macchiato Cookies   156

6
Old-Fashioned

Peanut Butter Pretzel Bites   161

Russian Tea Cakes   162

Homemade Oatmeal Chocolate Chip
    Cookies   165

Half-Moon Cookies   166

Old-Fashioned Pecan Pie Cheesecake Bars   169

Nana's Best Coconut Macaroons   170

Chewy Classic Oatmeal Raisin Cookies   173

Turtle Thumbprint Cookies   174

Chewy Molasses Cookies   177

Classic French Madeleines   178

3-Ingredient Old-Fashioned Shortbread
   Buttons   181

Breakfast Cookies   182

Red Velvet Thumbprints   185

Toffee Butter Icebox Cookies   186

Ricotta Cookies   189

Soft Peanut Butter Cookies   190

Acknowledgments   222

Index   223

About the Author   228

7
Holiday

3-Ingredient Pumpkin Cake Cookies   195

Christmas Magic Squares   196

Peppermint Crunch Balls   199

North Pole Lemon Cookies   200

Jolly Holly Cookies   203

Easy Pecan Pie Bars   204

Italian Christmas Cookies   207

Stained Glass Window Cookies   208

Chocolate Kiss Surprise Powder Puff Cookies   211

Pizzelles   212

Unforgettable White Chocolate Cranberry
   Cookies   215

Gingerbread People   216

Christmas Crinkles   219

So Easy Snowball Cookies   220

Introduction

Like many of us, I learned at a young age that cookies are special. They are a comfort we can come back to again and again in our hectic lives. Whether playful or sophisticated, chewy or crunchy, they always bring me back to my childhood and the sheer joy of being allowed to reach into the cookie jar for a tasty reward. Every time the heavenly aroma of a freshly baked batch of chocolate chip or oatmeal raisin cookies wafts through the air, I'm transported back to the first time I made my own cookies. I was in the kitchen at a friend's house, happily measuring out ingredients as instructed so that I could lick the spatula clean at the end. At the time, it was simply a fun activity to do on a playdate. It wasn't until I was old enough to follow a recipe on my own that I understood: Back then, I was learning to bake.

There's a French phrase, *mise en place*, that means "everything in its place." When I was young and helping my friend's mom bake chocolate chip cookies, I was learning how to lay things out and organize my ingredients. I've since come to realize that the success of a recipe almost always comes down to whether you are prepared. With the right preparation, the delightful and comforting treats in this book can be whipped up with no trouble at all.

I learned the importance of *mise en place* in culinary school, but it's a skill I use regularly in my home cooking and party planning. If everything is in place (which is usually what takes the most time!), then when guests arrive or the kids get home from school, there's not much left to do before everyone can enjoy the food you've prepared. Despite the seemingly rigid nature of measuring things out, this actually opens up more room for creativity. And cookie recipes function the same way. Once all the basic ingredients are in place, your mind is free to think of what you can add, what you can change, and how you can make them yours.

Baking is a science, and there is a formula to the ingredients you need to make a successful recipe. Once you have the basics down, you can swap out flavors, add nuts, change up the type of chocolate, dash in citrus, or top with sprinkles. Once you learn the basics, you can play. This book is a collection of 103 playful recipes that add to, change up, and make old recipes new and exciting, while maintaining what makes cookies classic. Why 103? When you come to our house for dinner or dessert, we want you to know you can always bring a friend, or two, or three. One hundred felt so rigid, and when experimenting with food, especially cookies, there is always room for three more.

—Addie Gundry

1

Bar Cookies

Bar cookies, including brownies and blondies, are a beautiful
hybrid between a cookie and a cake. Dense, chewy, and gooey,
baked thick and sliced into squares or rectangles, bar cookies are one
of my favorite desserts. This chapter is full of chocolate, sugar, caramel,
peanut butter, and more. Whether you're making them to
take on the road or to a bake sale, or to slice up and
serve at home, bar cookies just can't be beat.

Apple Pie Bars

Yield: 18 bars | Prep Time: 25 minutes | Cook Time: 40–45 minutes

Apple pie was always the crown jewel of my family's Thanksgiving table growing up. But who wants to wait a whole year to enjoy the melting together of crisp apples, cinnamon, brown sugar, and butter? With this recipe, you don't have to. I set out to create something that could mimic the experience of a classic apple pie but can be enjoyed on the weekday, in the morning, or for a late-night treat.

INGREDIENTS

1 cup (2 sticks) unsalted butter, softened

⅓ cup plus ½ cup granulated sugar

1 tablespoon sour cream

1 large egg

½ teaspoon kosher salt

2¼ cups all-purpose flour

3 Granny Smith apples, peeled, cored, and thinly sliced

1½ teaspoons ground cinnamon

¼ teaspoon ground cardamom

½ cup chopped walnuts

2 tablespoons light brown sugar

Vanilla ice cream for serving

DIRECTIONS

1. Preheat the oven to 350°F. Lightly coat a 9 × 13-inch baking dish with cooking spray.

2. In a large bowl, cream the unsalted butter and ⅓ cup of the granulated sugar with a whisk. Beat in the sour cream, egg, and salt. Stir in the flour and mix until a soft dough forms.

3. Spread half the dough into the bottom of the prepared baking dish, pressing down lightly into an even layer.

4. In another large bowl, combine the apples, ½ cup granulated sugar, 1 teaspoon of the cinnamon, and the cardamom.

5. Spread the apple mixture evenly over the dough in the baking dish and cover with the remaining dough.

6. In a small bowl, combine the walnuts, brown sugar, and remaining ½ teaspoon cinnamon. Sprinkle over the dough.

7. Bake for 40 to 45 minutes, until golden brown.

8. Cool in the baking dish, then cut into bars.

9. Serve with vanilla ice cream.

3-Layer Nanaimo Bars

Yield: 10 bars | Prep Time: 30 minutes plus 6 hours 30 minutes chilling time | Cook Time: n/a

I could snack on bananas, chocolate, or graham crackers all day long. Put them together, and the multiple textures and flavors get better with every bite. The creamy bananas with a graham cracker crunch satisfy my snack cravings every time. And who could say no to throwing some chocolate in the mix?

INGREDIENTS

Crust

½ cup (1 stick) unsalted butter

¼ cup granulated sugar

1 large egg, lightly beaten

1 teaspoon vanilla extract

1½ cups graham cracker crumbs

1 cup sweetened shredded coconut

½ cup chopped pecans

Filling

6 tablespoons (¾ stick) unsalted butter, softened

1 (3.4-ounce) package banana cream instant pudding mix

½ cup whole milk

3 cups confectioners' sugar

Topping

1 cup bittersweet chocolate chips

2 tablespoons unsalted butter

DIRECTIONS

1. *For the crust:* In a medium saucepan, melt the butter for the crust. Add the granulated sugar and stir until it has dissolved. Add the egg and vanilla, stir until combined well, and remove from the heat.

2. Add the graham cracker crumbs, coconut, and pecans and mix well.

3. Press the crust into an 8-inch square baking dish and refrigerate until ready to fill.

4. *For the filling:* In a large bowl, beat the butter until creamy. Add the pudding mix and the milk and mix until thickened.

5. Mix in the confectioners' sugar slowly until smooth.

6. Spread the pudding mixture over the refrigerated pie crust. Chill for 30 minutes.

7. *For the topping:* In a microwave-safe bowl, combine the chocolate chips and butter. Microwave for 15 to 20 seconds on high and stir. Microwave, stirring every 10 to 15 seconds, until the chocolate is melted and smooth.

8. Evenly pour the chocolate on top of the pudding layer.

9. Chill for 6 hours before cutting into bars or squares to serve.

Seven Layers of Heaven

Yield: 16 bars | Prep Time: 5 minutes | Cook Time: 30–40 minutes

There's just no way you can combine coconut, toffee, and chocolate and go wrong. Believe me, this bar is heaven in dessert form.

INGREDIENTS

½ cup (1 stick) unsalted butter

1 cup graham cracker crumbs

1 cup semisweet chocolate chips

1 cup toffee chips

1 cup coarsely chopped pecans, plus more for garnish

1 cup shredded coconut, plus more for garnish

1 (14-ounce) can sweetened condensed milk

DIRECTIONS

1. Preheat the oven to 350°F.

2. Place the butter into an 8-inch square baking dish and put it in the oven as it preheats. When the butter has melted, remove the dish from the oven.

3. Add the graham cracker crumbs to the baking dish and stir. Press the crumbs into an even layer in the bottom of the dish. Add separate, even layers of the following ingredients in this order: chocolate chips, toffee chips, pecans, coconut, and condensed milk.

4. Bake for 30 to 40 minutes. Remove from the oven and sprinkle with extra pecans and coconut.

5. Cool completely on a wire rack before cutting into bars to serve.

Five-Layer Chocolate Cherry Bars

Yield: 24 bars | Prep Time: 10 minutes | Cook Time: 25–30 minutes

I used to eat so many cherries when I was a kid that I'd stain my fingers red. I always knew the school year was almost over when I'd come home and my mom would have a bowl of these dark crimson beauties on the table. These Five-Layer Chocolate Cherry Bars bring me back to carefree childhood summers, no matter what time of year I make them.

INGREDIENTS

1½ cups graham cracker crumbs

½ cup (1 stick) unsalted butter, melted

1 cup dried cherries

1 cup semisweet chocolate chips

½ cup sweetened shredded coconut

1 (14-ounce) can sweetened condensed milk

½ cup sliced almonds

DIRECTIONS

1. Preheat the oven to 350°F. Lightly coat a 9 × 13-inch baking dish with cooking spray.

2. In a medium bowl, combine the graham cracker crumbs and melted butter, stirring completely until the mixture resembles wet sand. Press into the prepared baking dish in an even layer. Add separate, even layers of the following ingredients in this order: dried cherries, chocolate chips, coconut, condensed milk, and almonds.

3. Bake for 25–30 minutes, until golden brown. Cool completely on a wire rack before cutting into bars to serve.

Peanut Butter Bars

Yield: 24 bars | Prep Time: 10 minutes | Cook Time: 40 minutes

I find any and every excuse to eat as much peanut butter as possible, and this has rubbed off on my entire family (even our sweet puppy). Peanut Butter Bars are a family favorite that I highly recommend for getting your peanut butter fix.

INGREDIENTS

1 (15.25-ounce) package yellow cake mix

2 large eggs

1 cup creamy peanut butter

½ cup (1 stick) unsalted butter, melted

10 ounces peanut butter chips

1 (14-ounce) can sweetened condensed milk

½ cup dry-roasted unsalted peanuts

DIRECTIONS

1. Preheat the oven to 350°F. Lightly coat a 9 × 13-inch baking dish with cooking spray.

2. In a stand mixer fitted with the paddle attachment, combine the cake mix, eggs, peanut butter, and melted butter and mix on medium speed until well combined, about 2 minutes. Press approximately two-thirds of this mixture into the prepared baking dish, using your fingers to make an even layer. Bake for 10 minutes, until slightly dry on top. Remove from the oven.

3. Spread the peanut butter chips evenly over the baked bottom layer and pour the condensed milk on top. Use your fingers to make tablespoon-size scoops of the remaining batter and drop them randomly over the condensed milk layer. Sprinkle evenly with the peanuts. Bake for 30 minutes, until the top is golden brown and the center of the bars is firm. (The toothpick test will not work because of the sticky center layer.)

4. Cool on a wire rack completely before cutting into bars to serve.

Strawberry Cheesecake Bars

Yield: 24 bars | Prep Time: 20 minutes | Cook Time: 30–35 minutes

Throughout my career in cooking, I've noticed that many of my friends are intimidated by baking cheesecake. What I love about this recipe is how you get the same creamy indulgence with minimal fuss.

INGREDIENTS

1 (15.25-ounce) package Pillsbury Moist Supreme strawberry cake mix

½ cup (1 stick) unsalted butter, melted

3 large eggs

¾ cup strawberry jam

8 ounces cream cheese, at room temperature

1 teaspoon vanilla extract

Fresh strawberries, sliced (optional)

DIRECTIONS

1. Preheat the oven to 375°F. Lightly coat a 9 × 13-inch baking dish with cooking spray.

2. In a stand mixer fitted with the paddle attachment, combine the cake mix, melted butter, and 1 of the eggs. Mix on medium-high speed for 2 minutes, until all the ingredients are well combined; the batter will be very stiff.

3. Use your hands to press the batter in an even layer on the bottom and ½ inch up the sides of the prepared baking dish. Spread the strawberry jam over the batter in an even layer.

4. In the same stand mixer bowl, combine the cream cheese, the remaining 2 eggs, and the vanilla and mix on medium until completely smooth, about 3 minutes. Pour the cream cheese mixture into the baking dish, keeping it inside the raised edges of the bottom layer. Bake for 30 to 35 minutes, until the top is just beginning to brown and the cheesecake layer is almost firm in the center.

5. Cool completely on a wire rack. If not serving immediately, cover loosely with plastic wrap and refrigerate. Cut into bars or small squares to serve, garnishing each with a slice of fresh strawberry, if desired.

Peanut Butter Bacon Bars

Yield: 16 bars | Prep Time: 15 minutes | Cook Time: 20–25 minutes

Bacon is no longer just a breakfast food in my house. It makes for the perfect sweet-and-salty treat when mixed with peanut butter and chocolate. Careful—I know from experience how easy it is to get addicted to this devilish dessert.

INGREDIENTS

8 bacon slices

1½ cups all-purpose flour

1 teaspoon baking soda

Pinch of salt

1 cup packed light brown sugar

½ cup (1 stick) unsalted butter, softened

½ cup chunky peanut butter

1 large egg

1 teaspoon vanilla extract

1½ cups semisweet chocolate chips

½ cup coarsely chopped salted peanuts

DIRECTIONS

1. Preheat the oven to 350°F. Lightly coat a 9-inch square baking dish with cooking spray.

2. In a large skillet, cook the bacon until crispy. Drain the grease and chop the bacon coarsely. Set aside.

3. In a medium bowl, use a whisk to stir together the flour, baking soda, and salt.

4. In a stand mixer fitted with the paddle attachment, cream together the brown sugar and butter until light and fluffy, about 2 minutes. Add the peanut butter, egg, and vanilla and beat until smooth. Add the flour mixture and beat for 1 minute. By hand, stir in half the cooked bacon. Spread the batter into the prepared baking dish and bake for 20 to 25 minutes, until firm.

5. Remove the base from the oven, top with the chocolate chips, and return to the oven until the chocolate begins to melt, about 1 minute. Remove the baking dish from the oven. Spread the melted chips with a spatula to make an even layer of "frosting" and top with the remaining bacon and the peanuts. Cool completely before cutting into squares or bars to serve.

No-Bake Coconut Graham Cracker Cookie Bars

Yield: 16 bars | Prep Time: 25 minutes plus 4 hours chilling time | Cook Time: 5 minutes

The first time I made these, I was hosting a tropical tiki party, and they were the perfect sweet treat after homemade cocktails and spicy Caribbean-inspired food.

INGREDIENTS

Crust

1 (16-ounce) box graham crackers

¾ cup (1½ sticks) unsalted butter, softened

1 cup granulated sugar

1 large egg

½ cup whole milk

1 cup chopped walnuts

1 cup sweetened shredded coconut

½ teaspoon vanilla extract

Frosting

8 ounces cream cheese, softened

½ cup (1 stick) unsalted butter, softened

1 cup confectioners' sugar

1 teaspoon vanilla extract

2 tablespoons whole milk

DIRECTIONS

1. *For the crust:* Remove one sleeve of the graham crackers and finely crush in a food processor or by hand. Set aside with the remaining crackers, left whole.

2. In a large heavy saucepan, melt the butter over medium-low heat. In a separate bowl, combine the granulated sugar, egg, and milk and mix well. Whisk the mixture into the melted butter. Bring to a boil, whisking continuously until the mixture thickens, then remove from the heat.

3. Line the bottom of a 9 × 13-inch baking dish with a layer of whole graham crackers.

4. Stir the walnuts, shredded coconut, crushed crackers, and vanilla into the butter mixture and spoon it over the layer of crackers in the baking dish in a smooth layer. Top with another layer of whole graham crackers and press them gently into the filling.

5. *For the frosting:* In a stand mixer fitted with the paddle attachment, whip the cream cheese on medium-high until smooth. Add the butter and whip until fluffy, then gradually add the confectioners' sugar and vanilla. Stir in enough of the milk to make an easily spreadable frosting. Spread over the graham cracker layer using an offset spatula to make a smooth top.

6. Cover lightly with plastic wrap and chill for at least 4 hours or overnight to soften the layers. Keep in the refrigerator, and when ready to serve, remove from the refrigerator and cut into bars while cold.

Zebra Bars

Yield: 32–36 bars | Prep Time: 25 minutes | Cook Time: 25–30 minutes

These bars have so many mix-ins that they look like wild animals. Or in other words, their zebra stripes certainly show! Take your basic blondie and add white and milk chocolate to it, to create a stripy swirl.

INGREDIENTS

1 cup (2 sticks) unsalted butter, softened

1 cup packed light brown sugar

2 large eggs

1 teaspoon vanilla extract

2 cups all-purpose flour

1 teaspoon baking powder

1½ cups semisweet chocolate chips

½ cup white chocolate chips

¾ cup chopped pecans

DIRECTIONS

1. Preheat the oven to 350°F. Lightly coat a 9 × 13-inch baking dish with cooking spray.

2. In a stand mixer fitted with the paddle attachment, cream the butter and brown sugar until well mixed.

3. Beat in the eggs, vanilla, flour, and baking powder.

4. Put 1 cup of the semisweet chocolate chips in a medium microwave-safe bowl. Microwave on high in 30-second intervals, stirring after each, until melted.

5. Combine half the batter with the melted chocolate. Spread the chocolate batter over the bottom of the prepared baking dish.

6. Drop tablespoons of the remaining batter over the chocolate layer and drag a knife through the batter to create zebra stripes.

7. Sprinkle the remaining ½ cup semisweet chocolate chips, the white chocolate chips, and the pecans over the batter.

8. Bake for 25 to 30 minutes.

9. Let cool and cut into bars, or use a ring mold to cut into circles and serve.

Peanut Butter Swirl Bars

Yield: 24 bars | Prep Time: 15 minutes | Cook Time: 35 minutes

If peanut butter bars are not sweet enough, let's add a little chocolate and swirl! Get your chocolate and peanut butter fix with these groovy-looking and -tasting treats.

INGREDIENTS

½ cup creamy peanut butter

⅓ cup unsalted butter, softened

¾ cup packed light brown sugar

¾ cup granulated sugar

2 large eggs

2 teaspoons vanilla extract

1 cup self-rising flour

½ cup peanuts

1 cup semisweet chocolate chips

1 cup dark chocolate chips

DIRECTIONS

1. Preheat the oven to 350°F. Lightly coat a 9 × 13-inch baking dish with cooking spray.

2. In a stand mixer fitter with the wire whip, whisk together the peanut butter, butter, brown sugar, and granulated sugar until creamy. Add the eggs and vanilla and mix well.

3. Add the flour and blend in well. Fold in the peanuts.

4. Spread the batter into a 9 × 13-inch baking dish.

5. Sprinkle the semisweet chocolate chips and dark chocolate chips over the batter.

6. Bake for 5 minutes. Remove from the oven. Run a knife through the batter to swirl the melted chocolate.

7. Return to the oven and bake for an additional 30 minutes.

8. Cool, then cut into bars to serve.

Oatmeal Chocolate Raisin Bars

Yield: 24 bars | Prep Time: 20 minutes | Cook Time: 25–30 minutes

I love oatmeal-raisin cookies. I also love chocolate. When I can't quite decide between oatmeal-raisin and oatmeal-chocolate, I figure, why choose at all? Why not enjoy the best of both?

INGREDIENTS

1 cup (2 sticks) unsalted butter, softened

1 cup packed light brown sugar

½ cup granulated sugar

2 large eggs

2 teaspoons vanilla extract

½ teaspoon salt

1 teaspoon baking soda

1 teaspoon baking powder

1 teaspoon ground cinnamon

1½ cups all-purpose flour

2 cups rolled oats

¾ cup golden raisins

1 cup semisweet chocolate chips

1 cup dark chocolate chips

DIRECTIONS

1. Preheat the oven to 350°F. Lightly coat a 9 × 13-inch baking dish with cooking spray.

2. In a large bowl, cream together the butter, brown sugar, and granulated sugar until well combined. Add the eggs, then the vanilla.

3. Slowly add the salt, baking soda, baking powder, cinnamon, flour, oats, raisins, and semisweet chocolate chips.

4. Spread half the mixture in the prepared baking dish. Sprinkle the dark chocolate chips over the top. Spread the remaining oat mixture over the chocolate chips.

5. Bake for 25 to 30 minutes, until golden brown.

6. Cool, then cut into bars to serve.

Stir and Bake Bars

Yield: 24 bars | Prep Time: 10 minutes | Cook Time: 30 minutes

As much as I love baking, even I can admit that it can sometimes feel tedious. Who wants to get home after a long day at work and worry about frosting something perfectly? For those lazy days, this homemade dessert hardly feels like any work at all! You're still rewarded with a chocolaty masterpiece when it comes out of the oven.

INGREDIENTS

1 (15.25-ounce) package devil's food cake mix

1 cup sweetened shredded coconut

½ cup quick-cooking oats

½ cup packed light brown sugar

⅓ cup vegetable oil

⅓ cup water

2 large eggs

½ cup dark chocolate chips, plus extra for topping

½ cup coarsely chopped walnuts, plus extra for topping

DIRECTIONS

1. Preheat the oven to 350°F. Lightly coat a 9 × 13-inch baking dish with cooking spray.

2. In a large bowl, combine the cake mix, shredded coconut, oats, and brown sugar, stirring with a spatula or wooden spoon to break up any lumps.

3. In a medium bowl, combine the vegetable oil, water, and eggs and mix with a fork. Add to the dry ingredients and mix until well combined. Pour into the prepared baking dish, spreading it to the sides and corners in an even layer.

4. Sprinkle the dark chocolate chips and walnuts evenly over the top. Bake for 25 to 30 minutes; cool completely on a wire rack. Top with additional chocolate chips and walnuts, cut into squares, and serve.

Salted Caramel Bars

Yield: 24 bars │ Prep Time: 20 minutes plus 1 hour chilling time │ Cook Time: 5 minutes

Salty-sweet is a classic combo, but do you know why it's so darn good? When you take your first bite, the salt opens up your taste buds and gets them ready so the rest tastes extra good. That's why the caramel-y goodness of these bars is addictive.

INGREDIENTS

80 saltine or club crackers

1 cup (2 sticks) unsalted butter, softened

1 cup packed light brown sugar

½ cup whole milk

⅓ cup granulated sugar

1 teaspoon vanilla extract

1 cup semisweet chocolate chips

1 cup dark chocolate chips

1 cup almonds, toasted and chopped

Sea salt

DIRECTIONS

1. Line a 9 × 13-inch baking sheet with parchment paper, leaving an overhang.

2. Line the baking sheet with a layer of crackers, cutting them to fit if needed.

3. In a medium saucepan, melt the butter. Add the brown sugar, milk, granulated sugar, and vanilla. Bring to a boil, then cook, stirring continuously, for 5 minutes.

4. Remove from the heat and pour half the mixture over the crackers.

5. Place another layer of crackers over the butter-sugar mixture. Pour the remaining butter-sugar mixture over the crackers. Top with a final layer of crackers.

6. Put the semisweet chocolate chips and dark chocolate chips in a medium microwave-safe bowl. Microwave on high in 30-second intervals, stirring after each, until melted. (Alternatively, melt the chocolate in a saucepan on the stovetop.)

7. Pour the melted chocolate over the crackers and spread it evenly.

8. Top with the toasted almonds and a bit of sea salt.

9. Chill for at least 1 hour before cutting into bars to serve.

Trillionaire Dessert Bars

Yield: 9–12 bars | Prep Time: 30–45 minutes | Cook Time: 35 minutes

Ever had a dessert that trumps all others? You take one bite and think that even if you were living in a palace, hosting dignitaries from around the world, you'd still want to be serving that dessert. That's what this dessert is. It's the one you'd want to enjoy in a mansion, at a block party, or even in your office kitchen. It's that good.

INGREDIENTS

Brownie Layer

1 (18.3-ounce) package brownie mix

Caramel Layer

1 cup store-bought bourbon caramel sauce

Cookie Dough Layer

½ cup (1 stick) unsalted butter, softened

½ cup packed light brown sugar

¼ cup granulated sugar

½ teaspoon vanilla extract

2 tablespoons heavy cream

¾ cup all-purpose flour

⅛ teaspoon sea salt

¼ cup dark chocolate chips

¼ cup mini semisweet chocolate chips

Chocolate Glaze

1 cup dark chocolate chips

2 tablespoons heavy cream

DIRECTIONS

1. *For the brownie layer:* Bake the brownie mix in an 8-inch square baking dish according to the package directions.

2. *For the caramel layer:* In a medium microwave-safe bowl, microwave the caramel sauce for 10 to 15 seconds. Pour the caramel over the brownie base. Refrigerate while you prepare the cookie dough base.

3. *For the cookie dough layer:* In a large bowl, cream together the butter, brown sugar, and granulated sugar until light. Mix in the vanilla and cream. Add the flour and sea salt and mix well. Stir in the dark chocolate chips and semisweet chocolate chips.

4. When the caramel layer on the brownie base has firmed up, about 5 minutes, carefully spread the cookie dough evenly over the caramel layer.

5. *For the chocolate glaze:* In a small microwave-safe bowl, combine the chocolate chips and cream. Microwave for 1 minute, then stir. Microwave for 20-second intervals, stirring after each, until the chocolate is melted.

6. Spread the melted chocolate over the cookie dough layer. Let it set, then cut it into bars to serve.

Dreamboat Caramel Bars

Yield: 15 bars | Prep Time: 20 minutes | Cook Time: 25 minutes

Take classic caramel candies to the next level with these gooey and delicious bars. The feel of each bite melting in your mouth is so good, you'll be fantasizing about it long after the batch is gone.

INGREDIENTS

Bottom Layer

2¼ cups all-purpose flour

1 teaspoon baking soda

1 teaspoon salt

1 cup (2 sticks) unsalted butter, softened

¾ cup granulated sugar

¾ cup packed light brown sugar

1 teaspoon vanilla extract

2 large eggs

Top Layer

1 (5-ounce) can evaporated milk

14 whole soft caramel candies, unwrapped

½ cup creamy peanut butter

1 cup (6 ounces) chocolate baking chunks or chips

DIRECTIONS

1. *For the bottom layer:* Preheat the oven to 375°F. Lightly coat a 9 × 13-inch baking dish with cooking spray.

2. In a large bowl, combine the flour, baking soda, and salt and toss with a fork to mix well.

3. In a stand mixer fitted with the paddle attachment, combine the butter, granulated sugar, and brown sugar and beat on medium-high speed for 2 to 3 minutes, until light and creamy. Turn the machine off and scrape down the bowl. Turn the machine back on, and with the machine running, add the vanilla and eggs, one at a time, and then gradually add the flour mixture.

4. Spread half the dough into the prepared baking dish, pressing it into an even layer. Bake for 8 minutes—the layer will be slightly firm but not fully baked.

5. *For the top layer:* While the bottom layer bakes, put the evaporated milk and caramel candies in a small, heavy saucepan and cook over low heat, stirring frequently, until the caramels have melted and the mixture is smooth. Remove from the heat and stir in the peanut butter until smooth.

6. Remove the pan from the oven and spread the caramel mixture over the bottom layer in an even layer. Sprinkle with the chocolate baking chunks and then add the remaining dough by spoonfuls over the top. Return the pan to the oven and bake for 15 to 20 minutes, until the top is golden brown. (You will not be able to test this with a toothpick, as the center will be very soft and gooey.)

7. Cool completely on a wire rack before cutting into squares to serve.

Chocolate Peanut Butter Bars

Yield: 24 bars | Prep Time: 10 minutes | Cook Time: 5 minutes

These remind me of the bake sale I used to help out with when I was a kid. Someone always made chocolate peanut butter bars because they're such a timeless favorite. This recipe is so simple and delivers every time.

INGREDIENTS

Crust

1 cup creamy peanut butter

1 cup (2 sticks) unsalted butter, softened

4 cups confectioners' sugar

¾ cup graham cracker crumbs

½ cup coarsely chopped peanuts

Topping

1 (11-ounce) package peanut butter–milk chocolate chips (see Note)

½ cup heavy whipping cream

½ cup coarsely chopped peanuts

DIRECTIONS

1. *For the crust:* Line a 9 × 13-inch baking dish with parchment paper or waxed paper, leaving a 2-inch overhang on both long sides.

2. In a stand mixer fitted with the paddle attachment, combine the creamy peanut butter and butter and beat on medium speed until smooth. With the machine running, gradually add the confectioners' sugar and graham cracker crumbs until combined. Stir in the peanuts.

3. Spread the crust mixture into the prepared pan and press it into the corners into an even layer with your fingers.

4. *For the topping:* In a small, heavy saucepan, combine the peanut butter–milk chocolate chips and cream and heat over low heat, stirring, until the chips have melted and the mixture is smooth. Spread over the crust using an offset spatula to make a smooth layer. Sprinkle with the peanuts. Chill, uncovered, in the refrigerator for 20 minutes before cutting to serve, or cover lightly and refrigerate for up to 2 days.

5. When ready to serve, use the overhanging parchment paper to lift the bars from the pan in one piece and let stand for 10 minutes before cutting into bars. Store any leftovers in the refrigerator.

NOTE

If peanut butter–milk chocolate chips are not available in your store, combine ¾ cup chocolate chips with ¾ cup peanut butter chips—or use 11 ounces chocolate chips, if necessary.

Texas Gold Bars

Yield: 24 bars | Prep Time: 20 minutes | Cook Time: 40–45 minutes

You'll know you've struck gold as soon as you take a bite out of these decadent cookie bars. The cream cheese makes these sweets so addicting. They're named Texas Gold Bars because their golden hue looks like something right out of the Wild West!

INGREDIENTS

1 (15.25-ounce) box lemon cake mix

1 cup (2 sticks) unsalted butter, melted

3 large eggs

4 ounces cream cheese, softened

4 ounces mascarpone cheese, softened

2 teaspoons vanilla extract

1 teaspoon lemon zest

16 ounces confectioners' sugar

DIRECTIONS

1. Preheat the oven to 350°F. Lightly coat a 9 × 13-inch baking dish with cooking spray.

2. In a stand mixer fitted with the paddle attachment, combine the lemon cake mix, half the melted butter, and 1 of the eggs. Mix until a consistency of cookie dough is reached.

3. Press into the bottom of the baking dish in an even layer.

4. In a large bowl, beat the cream cheese and mascarpone cheese until smooth. Add the remaining 2 eggs, remaining melted butter, the vanilla, and the lemon zest. Mix well.

5. Slowly add the confectioners' sugar, scraping the bowl down as you go, until light and fluffy.

6. Pour the mixture over the cake base.

7. Bake for 40 to 45 minutes, until the top is lightly golden and the crust is starting to crack.

8. Cool and cut into bars to serve.

Raspberry Oatmeal Cookie Bars

Yield: 9–12 bars | Prep Time: 15 minutes | Cook Time: 34–38 minutes

These bars are great any time of day! That's right, even in the morning. They're one of my favorite things to make for brunch, since the raspberries and oatmeal add a fruity, healthy kick to a sweet treat.

INGREDIENTS

1 cup all-purpose flour

¼ teaspoon baking soda

¼ teaspoon kosher salt

¼ teaspoon ground cinnamon

1 cup rolled oats

½ cup packed dark brown sugar

½ cup (1 stick) unsalted butter, softened

¾ cup raspberry jam (seedless, if desired)

¼ cup sliced almonds

½ cup confectioners' sugar

1 tablespoon whole milk

½–1 teaspoon vanilla extract

DIRECTIONS

1. Preheat the oven to 350°F. Line an 8-inch square baking dish with parchment paper, leaving a 2-inch overhang on two sides of the dish. Lightly coat with cooking spray.

2. In a large bowl, combine the flour, baking soda, salt, and cinnamon. Mix in the rolled oats and brown sugar. Use a fork or your fingertips to form crumbs.

3. Work the butter into the oat mixture with your hands until moistened.

4. Press 2 cups, loosely measured, of the mixture into the prepared baking dish.

5. Spread the jam in an even layer over the oat mixture. Sprinkle the remaining oat mixture over the jam, then press down lightly. Sprinkle the almonds over the top.

6. Bake for 34 to 38 minutes. Remove from the oven and cool.

7. In a small bowl, mix the confectioners' sugar with the milk until smooth. Add the vanilla. Drizzle over the top of the crumb bars. Cut into bars to serve.

Better-Than-Anything Scotcharoos

Yield: 32–36 bars | Prep Time: 15 minutes | Cook Time: n/a

These are the perfect treat for a birthday party. The combination of crispy rice cereal, peanut butter, chocolate, and brightly colored sprinkles is every kid's dream. Whip these together in no time, making them a quick treat to add to a big day!

INGREDIENTS

Butter for greasing the baking dish

1 cup sugar

1 cup corn syrup

1 cup crunchy peanut butter

½ cup toffee chips

6 cups crispy rice cereal

1 (12-ounce) bag semisweet chocolate chips

1 (11-ounce) bag butterscotch chips

Multi-colored sprinkles for topping

DIRECTIONS

1. Butter a 9 × 13-inch baking dish.

2. In a large saucepan, combine the sugar and corn syrup. Bring to a boil over medium heat, stirring to dissolve the sugar. Remove from the heat and stir in the peanut butter.

3. Add the toffee chips. Add the crispy rice cereal and mix well. Press the mixture into the prepared baking dish.

4. In a large microwave-safe bowl, combine the semisweet chocolate chips and butterscotch chips. Microwave in 30-second intervals, stirring after each, until melted and smooth.

5. Pour the chocolate-butterscotch mixture over the crispy rice cereal mixture and smooth the top.

6. Cool and add sprinkles on top before cutting into bars to serve.

2

Cake Mix Cookies

When I first found out I could use cake mix to create
doughnuts, cookies, and more, I was beyond excited. What a
brilliant "hack" to make a delicious semi-homemade
treat. Here are almost a dozen recipes that save you time
but don't compromise on flavor or appearance!

Chocolate Cake Mix Cookies

Yield: 36 cookies | Prep Time: 20 minutes | Cook Time: 10–12 minutes

When friends and family ask you the secret to making the fluffiest cookies around, you'll just have to smile 'cause you know it's all in the cake mix! Feel free to try out other cake mix flavors that catch your eye to customize this recipe to fit your whim.

INGREDIENTS

1 (16.25-ounce) package devil's food cake mix

2 large eggs

½ (8-ounce) container frozen whipped topping, thawed

¼ teaspoon instant espresso powder

½ cup mini semisweet chocolate chips

½ cup confectioners' sugar, plus extra for dusting

DIRECTIONS

1. Preheat the oven to 350°F. Line two baking sheets with parchment paper.

2. In a stand mixer fitted with the paddle attachment, combine the cake mix, eggs, whipped topping, espresso powder, and chocolate chips. Mix on medium-high for 3 minutes, until well combined, pausing once to scrape down the sides and bottom of the bowl. The dough will be very sticky.

3. Put the confectioners' sugar in a small bowl. Dust your hands with some of the confectioners' sugar and shape the dough into ¾-inch balls. (Alternatively, use a cookie scoop to shape the dough.)

4. Coat the dough balls with confectioners' sugar and place them 2 inches apart on the prepared baking sheets.

5. Bake for 10 to 12 minutes, until the cookies are set and the tops have cracked.

6. Cool the cookies on a wire rack for about 10 minutes. Dust with additional confectioners' sugar, if desired. Serve.

Whipped Lemon Cookies

Yield: 40 cookies | Prep Time: 15 minutes | Cook Time: 8–10 minutes

Lemon desserts always remind me of springtime. They're so light and fresh and give you that extra pep. I love whipping these together anytime I need a little pick-me-up on a gloomy day!

INGREDIENTS

1 (15.25-ounce) lemon cake mix

2 cups frozen whipped topping, thawed

1 large egg

1 teaspoon lemon zest

1 cup confectioners' sugar

DIRECTIONS

1. Preheat the oven to 350°F. Line two baking sheets with parchment paper.

2. In a stand mixer fitted with the paddle attachment, combine the cake mix, whipped topping, egg, and lemon zest. Mix on medium-high speed for 3 minutes, until well combined, pausing once to scrape down the sides and bottom of the bowl.

3. Put the confectioners' sugar in a small bowl. Using a cookie scoop, shape the dough into 1-inch balls. Roll each ball in the confectioners' sugar and place them on the prepared baking sheets 1½ inches apart. Bake for 8 to 10 minutes, until the cookies are lightly golden brown.

4. Cool completely on a wire rack for 10 to 15 minutes before removing from the pans and storing in plastic storage containers . . . or eating!

10-Minute Miracle Cookies

Yield: 24 cookies | Prep Time: 10 minutes | Cook Time: 8–10 minutes

It's 10 p.m., and you just realized you forgot to prep a dessert for the bake sale in the morning. If you're looking for a miracle, you've got one in this recipe. Using only five ingredients and requiring only 10 minutes to prep, these cookies will get you out of a dessert jam with style!

INGREDIENTS

1 (15.25-ounce) package cake mix, any flavor

2 large eggs

⅓ cup vegetable oil

Granulated sugar for pressing cookies

Silver sugar pearls for garnish (optional)

DIRECTIONS

1. Preheat the oven to 375°F. Line two baking sheets with parchment paper.

2. In a medium bowl using a hand mixer or wooden spoon, mix the cake mix, eggs, and vegetable oil.

3. Using a cookie scoop, shape the dough into 1-inch balls and place on the prepared baking sheets about 2 inches apart. Dip a flat-bottomed glass into the sugar and press each ball of dough to a thickness of ¼ inch.

4. Bake for 8 to 10 minutes. Cool slightly and top with silver sugar pearls, if using, before transferring to a wire rack to cool completely before serving.

Easy Oatmeal Cookies

Yield: 36 cookies | Prep Time: 15 minutes | Cook Time: 12 minutes

This is the cookie recipe I always come back to again and again when whipping up treats for my family. The oats make the grownups feel okay about indulging in dessert while the chocolate convinces the kids to give them a try.

INGREDIENTS

1 (18.5-ounce) box yellow cake mix

2 cups quick-cooking oats

1 cup sugar

1 cup vegetable oil

2 large eggs

1 cup chopped walnuts

½ cup semisweet chocolate chips

1½ teaspoons vanilla extract

DIRECTIONS

1. Preheat the oven to 350°F. Line two baking sheets with parchment paper.

2. In a large bowl, combine the cake mix, oats, and sugar. In another small bowl, whisk together the vegetable oil and eggs.

3. Add the oil mixture to the cake mix mixture. Stir in the walnuts, chocolate chips, and vanilla.

4. Using a cookie scoop, shape the dough into 1-inch balls and place on the prepared baking sheets 2 inches apart. Bake for 12 minutes, until lightly browned.

5. Cool for 2 to 3 minutes, then transfer to a wire rack to cool for about 10 minutes. Serve.

VARIATIONS

Add raisins, dried cranberries, or dried cherries to the batter. You can also use white chocolate, butterscotch, or toffee chips instead of or in addition to the chocolate chips, or different nuts, such as pecans or cashews.

Lemon Pie Bars

Yield: 24 bars | Prep Time: 5 minutes | Cook Time: 20–25 minutes

Lemon squares are a favorite bakery treat of mine, and now I can bake this new-and-improved version in my own kitchen. It's much easier than traditional lemon squares but with the same iconic citrusy sweetness.

INGREDIENTS

1 (16-ounce) lemon cake mix

½ cup (1 stick) unsalted butter, softened

1 (21-ounce) can lemon pie filling

Sprinkles for garnish (optional)

DIRECTIONS

1. Preheat the oven to 350°F. Lightly coat a 9 × 13-inch baking dish with cooking spray.

2. In a stand mixer fitted with the paddle attachment, combine the cake mix and butter and beat on medium speed until well combined and crumbly. Set aside ½ cup of the mixture, and press the remaining mixture into the bottom of the prepared baking dish. Spoon the lemon pie filling over the top, spreading it into an even layer. Sprinkle the reserved dry mixture over the pie filling.

3. Bake for 20 to 25 minutes, until the filling is bubbling and the top begins to lightly brown.

4. Remove from oven and top with sprinkles (optional).

5. Cool completely on a wire rack before cutting into squares or bars to serve. Store any leftover bars, tightly covered, in the refrigerator.

Gooey Magic Cake Bars

Yield: 24 bars | Prep Time: 15 minutes | Cook Time: 24–28 minutes

Something magical always seems to be brewing when we've got a gooey coconut dessert on our hands. You'll need to stock up on extra napkins, but believe me, this decadent treat is well worth it!

INGREDIENTS

1 (15.25-ounce) box white cake mix

½ cup (1 stick) unsalted butter, softened

1 large egg

½ teaspoon vanilla extract

1 tablespoon water

1 cup sweetened shredded coconut

1 cup chopped macadamia nuts

1½ cups white chocolate chips

1 (14-ounce) can sweetened condensed milk

DIRECTIONS

1. Preheat the oven to 350°F. Line a 9 × 13-inch baking dish with parchment paper, then coat the paper with cooking spray.

2. In a large bowl, combine the cake mix, butter, egg, vanilla, and water. The dough will be very thick; use your hands to knead the dough if necessary.

3. Press the dough along the bottom and slightly up the sides of the prepared baking dish.

4. Sprinkle the shredded coconut evenly over the dough, then sprinkle with the macadamia nuts, and finally the white chocolate chips.

5. Pour the condensed milk over the chocolate chips.

6. Bake for 24 to 28 minutes, until the edges begin to lightly brown. Do not overbake.

7. Cool, then cut into bars to serve.

Chocolate Chip Bars

Yield: 18 bars | Prep Time: 20 minutes | Cook Time: 30–35 minutes

These aren't just ordinary chocolate chip bars. The mix-ins elevate this dessert to a whole different level. With two different kinds of chocolate and a nutty crunch for some texture, you'll be glad you gave this special cookie a chance!

INGREDIENTS

½ cup semisweet chocolate chips

½ cup dark chocolate chips

1 cup chopped walnuts

3 tablespoons dark brown sugar

1 (18.25-ounce) package yellow cake mix

½ cup (1 stick) unsalted butter, softened

2 large eggs

1 teaspoon vanilla extract

DIRECTIONS

1. Preheat the oven to 350°F. Lightly coat a 9 × 13-inch baking dish with cooking spray.

2. In a medium bowl, combine the semisweet chocolate chips, dark chocolate chips, walnuts, and brown sugar.

3. In a large bowl using a hand mixer, beat the cake mix, butter, eggs, and vanilla until well combined.

4. Stir half the chocolate chip mixture into the cake batter. Spread the batter over the bottom of the prepared baking dish. Sprinkle the remaining chocolate chip mixture over the batter.

5. Bake for 30 to 35 minutes, until set.

6. Cool, then cut into bars to serve.

M&M's Drop Cookies

Yield: 12–18 large cookies | Prep Time: 5 minutes | Cook Time: 10–12 minutes

When I was a kid, a big plate of M&M's cookies would appear in the kitchen before having guests and throwing a party. There's something intrinsically festive about all the bright colors. The M&M's baking bits come in a holiday version, too, so don't forget to revisit this one when December rolls around.

INGREDIENTS

1 (18-ounce) package white cake mix

⅓ cup vegetable oil

2 large eggs

½ teaspoon vanilla extract

Pinch of salt

¾ cup miniature M&M's baking bits, plus extra for decoration

DIRECTIONS

1. Preheat the oven to 350°F. Line two baking sheets with parchment paper.

2. In a stand mixer fitted with the paddle attachment, beat together the cake mix, vegetable oil, eggs, vanilla, and salt until well blended, about 3 minutes. Stir in the M&M's baking bits.

3. Using a cookie scoop, shape the dough into 1-inch balls and place on the prepared baking sheets about 2 inches apart. Sprinkle a few more M&M's baking bits on top to decorate.

4. Bake for 10 to 12 minutes, or until lightly golden around the edges.

5. Cool for 3 to 4 minutes, then transfer to a wire rack to cool completely. Serve, or store in an airtight container until ready to serve.

Cake Mix Magic Cream Cheese Squares

Yield: 24 squares | Prep Time: 10 minutes | Cook Time: 35 minutes

It's cream cheese to the rescue, once again! These cake mix squares have a magic all their own thanks to the fluffy combination of cake mix and cream cheese. I used yellow cake mix here, but feel free to substitute chocolate if you're in the mood.

INGREDIENTS

1 (15.25-ounce) package yellow cake mix

Vegetable oil and eggs as needed for the cake mix

¼ cup packed light brown sugar

⅓ cup unsalted butter, melted

8 ounces cream cheese, at room temperature

¼ cup granulated sugar

1 teaspoon vanilla extract

¾ cup finely chopped walnuts or almonds

DIRECTIONS

1. Preheat the oven to 350°F. Lightly coat a 9 × 13-inch baking dish with cooking spray.

2. Prepare the cake mix batter according to the package directions.

3. In a stand mixer fitted with the paddle attachment, combine the cake mix batter and brown sugar and beat on medium speed until well mixed. Add the melted butter and beat for 1 minute. Remove 1 cup of the mixture and set aside. Transfer the remaining mixture to the prepared pan and press to cover the bottom and slightly up the sides of the pan. Bake for 8 minutes—the crust will not be brown at this point, but it will be puffy.

4. In the same mixer bowl, combine the cream cheese, granulated sugar, and vanilla and beat on medium speed for 2 minutes, scraping the bowl once. When the crust comes out of the oven, pour the cream cheese mixture over it and spread it to the edges. Sprinkle with the reserved crumb mixture and chopped nuts and bake for 25 minutes until slightly crisp along the edges.

5. Cool completely on a wire rack before cutting into squares. Store the bars in the refrigerator, lightly covered, for up to 5 days.

10-Minute Cool Whip Cookies

Yield: 24–30 cookies | Prep Time: 10 minutes | Cook Time: 10 minutes

Whipped topping can make any dessert feel sophisticated, even if it's just Cool Whip. The airy buoyancy and creamy, melt-in-your-mouth texture combined with the light fluffiness of the cake cookie makes me feel like I'm having tea with the Queen of England.

INGREDIENTS

1 (8-ounce) container frozen whipped topping, thawed

2 large eggs

1 (18.25-ounce) package white cake mix

¼ cup sprinkles, plus extra for topping

⅓ cup confectioners' sugar

DIRECTIONS

1. Preheat the oven to 350°F. Lightly coat two baking sheets with cooking spray.

2. In a large bowl, beat together the whipped topping and the eggs. Add the cake mix and ¼ cup sprinkles and mix until well combined.

3. Put the confectioners' sugar in a small bowl. Using a cookie scoop, shape the dough into 1-inch balls and roll them in the confectioners' sugar to coat. Place the dough balls on the prepared baking sheets about 2 inches apart, top with additional sprinkles, and bake for 10 minutes.

4. Cool on a wire rack for 10 minutes before serving.

Funfetti Cake Batter Cookies

Yield: 12–18 cookies | Prep Time: 5 minutes | Cook Time: 6–8 minutes

Sprinkles are bright and colorful tidbits that evoke so many memories. Why not spread a little extra cheer the next time you want some cookies with these Funfetti Cake Batter Cookies? The box of cake mix plus a few special touches keeps them super easy while adding a "made from scratch" taste.

INGREDIENTS

1 (18-ounce) package Funfetti cake mix

⅓ cup vegetable oil

2 large eggs

1 teaspoon vanilla extract

Pinch of salt

Granulated sugar for sprinkling

Store-bought cream cheese frosting

Sprinkles

DIRECTIONS

1. Preheat the oven to 375°F. Line two baking sheets with parchment paper.

2. In a stand mixer fitted with the paddle attachment, beat together the cake mix, vegetable oil, eggs, vanilla, and salt for about 3 minutes, until well blended.

3. Using a cookie scoop, shape the dough into 1½-inch balls and place them on the prepared baking sheets 2 inches apart. Generously sprinkle the tops with granulated sugar and flatten gently with the bottom of a glass until about ⅓ inch thick.

4. Bake for 6 to 8 minutes, or until slightly golden around the edges.

5. Cool for 3 to 4 minutes, then transfer to a wire rack to cool completely. Once cool, frost with cream cheese frosting and top with sprinkles. Serve, or store in an airtight container until ready to serve for up to 5 days.

3

Fruits and Nuts

Adding fruits and nuts to a cookie boosts its flavor and makes
for a delightfully filling treat. The texture is also awesome,
with both crunchy and chewy elements adding to the tastiness
of the cookie. The recipes in this chapter all have delicious,
healthy characteristics that make for super fun cookies.

No-Bake Cookie Clusters

Yield: 28–30 cookies | Prep Time: 15 minutes plus 30 minutes chilling time | Cook Time: n/a

This recipe is perfect for making alongside young kids if they're looking to help you out in the kitchen! Everyone's hands might get a little sticky from the peanut butter and marshmallows, but it's well worth it.

INGREDIENTS

1 (12-ounce) package white chocolate chips

2 tablespoons creamy peanut butter

1¼ cups crispy rice cereal

1 cup cashews

1 cup mini marshmallows

DIRECTIONS

1. In a large saucepan, combine the white chocolate chips and peanut butter and heat over low heat, stirring continuously, until smooth. Remove from the heat and cool slightly until the mixture has thickened slightly.

2. Stir in the crispy rice cereal and cashews. Fold in the marshmallows.

3. Line two baking sheets with waxed paper. Using a cookie scoop, shape the dough into 1-inch balls and place them on the prepared baking sheets about 2 inches apart.

4. Chill in the fridge for 30 minutes until firm before serving.

Orange Cream Bars

Yield: 12 bars | Prep Time: 15–20 minutes | Cook Time: 20–25 minutes

This recipe reminds me of those orange Creamsicles I loved getting from the ice cream truck when I was little. And with these, you don't have to deal with a melted Popsicle running down your arm.

INGREDIENTS

Bars

1 (16.5-ounce) box orange cake mix

1 (3.4-ounce) package French vanilla instant pudding mix

2 large eggs

½ cup vegetable oil

¾ cup white chocolate chips

Frosting

8 ounces cream cheese, softened

½ cup (1 stick) unsalted butter, softened

2 cups confectioners' sugar

1 teaspoon orange zest

DIRECTIONS

1. *For the bars:* Preheat the oven to 350°F. Lightly coat a 9 × 13-inch baking dish with cooking spray.

2. In a large bowl, combine the cake mix, pudding mix, eggs, and vegetable oil and beat until a dough forms.

3. Stir in the white chocolate chips.

4. Press the dough into the bottom of the prepared baking dish.

5. Bake for 20 to 25 minutes, until golden and set. Cool.

6. *For the frosting:* In a medium bowl, beat the cream cheese and butter until well combined. Slowly add the confectioners' sugar and beat until smooth. Add the orange zest and mix.

7. Spread the frosting over the cookies and cut into bars. Serve.

Pecan Sandies

Yield: 36 cookies | Prep Time: 10 minutes plus 30 minutes chilling time | Cook Time: 20 minutes

The crispy butter flavor of these Pecan Sandies is too good to have only on special occasions. I like to keep a batch at the ready for when I get my next craving.

INGREDIENTS

¾ cup (1½ sticks) unsalted butter, softened

½ cup packed light brown sugar

¼ teaspoon kosher salt

¼ teaspoon ground nutmeg

2 cups all-purpose flour

1 cup finely chopped pecans

1½ teaspoons vanilla extract

DIRECTIONS

1. Preheat the oven to 325°F. Line two baking sheets with parchment paper.

2. In a stand mixer fitted with the paddle attachment or in a large bowl using a hand mixer, cream the butter and brown sugar until well combined.

3. Add the salt, nutmeg, flour, pecans, and vanilla and mix well to combine.

4. Chill the dough in the refrigerator for 30 minutes.

5. Using a cookie scoop, shape the dough into 1-inch balls and place on the prepared baking sheet about 2 inches apart.

6. Flatten each cookie ball to ½-inch thickness using the bottom of a flat glass.

7. Bake for 20 minutes.

8. Cool on a wire rack. Serve.

Strawberry Bars

Yield: 18 bars | Prep Time: 15 minutes | Cook Time: 35–40 minutes

Sometimes, I get a little jam crazy in the summer. Friends like to give jars away as cute home-made gifts, and it's so hard to resist those adorable stands on the side of the road. This is one of my favorite recipes to turn to when I've gone a bit overboard and have half-empty jam jars to use up.

INGREDIENTS

1 cup old-fashioned rolled oats

¾ cup all-purpose flour

⅓ cup packed light brown sugar

¼ teaspoon ground cinnamon

¼ teaspoon salt

6 tablespoons (¾ stick) unsalted butter, melted

1 cup all-fruit, no-added-sugar strawberry jelly or jam

DIRECTIONS

1. Preheat the oven to 375°F. Lightly coat an 8-inch square baking dish with cooking spray.

2. In a medium bowl, stir together the oats, flour, brown sugar, cinnamon, and salt until mixed and no lumps of brown sugar remain. Stir in the melted butter until well combined. Remove ½ cup of this mixture and set aside. Press the remainder evenly into the bottom of the prepared baking dish. Spread the jelly or jam evenly over the dough and sprinkle with the reserved dry mixture.

3. Bake for 35 to 40 minutes.

4. Cool completely on a wire rack before cutting into bars to serve.

2-Ingredient Lemon Bars

Yield: 24 bars | Prep Time: 5 minutes | Cook Time: 30 minutes

Yes, you read that right. There are only two ingredients needed to make this recipe. Skeptical? There's no need to be. Two ingredients truly are all you need to whip up a dessert you'll never forget!

INGREDIENTS

1 (16-ounce) box angel food cake mix (one-step, "add water" type)

22 ounces lemon pie filling

Confectioners' sugar (optional)

DIRECTIONS

1. Preheat the oven to 350°F. Lightly coat a 9 × 13-inch baking dish with cooking spray.

2. In a large bowl, combine the cake mix and the lemon pie filling.

3. Pour the batter into the prepared baking dish. Bake for 30 minutes, until lightly golden.

4. Cut into bars or use a ring mold and cut into circles. Serve dusted with confectioners' sugar, if you wish.

Chocolate Cherry Blossom Cookies

Yield: 30–36 cookies | Prep Time: 20 minutes | Cook Time: 12–15 minutes

George Washington may have had his famed cherry tree, but you, my friend, will be famous in your neighborhood for your unbelievable cherry cookies. By combining that fruity flavor with rich milk chocolate kisses, you've got a dish that's almost sinfully good.

INGREDIENTS

1 (10-ounce) jar stemless maraschino cherries

1 cup (2 sticks) unsalted butter, softened

1 cup confectioners' sugar

2¼ cups all-purpose flour

¼ teaspoon almond extract

2–3 drops liquid red food coloring

¼ cup granulated sugar

1 (12-ounce) bag milk chocolate kisses

DIRECTIONS

1. Preheat the oven to 350°F. Line two baking sheets with parchment paper.

2. Drain the maraschino cherries, reserving 1 tablespoon of the cherry juice from the jar. Coarsely chop the cherries–you should have about 1 cup chopped cherries.

3. In a stand mixer fitted with the paddle attachment, cream the butter on medium-high speed until smooth, then add the confectioners' sugar and beat until light and fluffy, about 3 minutes. With the mixer on medium-low, gradually add the flour, scraping down the bowl once, until all the flour has been absorbed. With the machine running, add the almond extract and just enough red food coloring to make a medium pink dough. Fold in the chopped cherries by hand.

4. Pour the granulated sugar into a small bowl. Using a cookie scoop, shape the dough into 1-inch balls and roll them in the sugar. Place on the baking sheets about 2 inches apart and press lightly with the bottom of a glass or measuring cup to make 1½-inch rounds. Bake for 12 to 15 minutes, until firm and the bottoms just begin to brown.

5. Cool on a wire rack for 2 minutes. Then press one milk chocolate kiss in the center of each cookie. Cool completely before moving or storing. Serve.

No-Bake Almond Coconut Cookies

Yield: 16 cookies | Prep Time: 10 minutes | Cook Time: 10 minutes, plus 2 to 3 hours sitting time

That's right—it's a candy bar favorite in a bring-along cookie form! When you've got crunchy almond and coconut flakes combined with the rich, creamy texture of chocolate hazelnut spread, there's no way you can go wrong.

INGREDIENTS

2 tablespoons unsalted butter

2 tablespoons heavy cream

½ cup chocolate-hazelnut spread

¼ teaspoon coconut extract

1 tablespoon unsweetened cocoa powder

1 cup sliced almonds

1½ cups sweetened shredded coconut

¾ cup quick-cooking oats

Pinch of sea salt

16 whole almonds

½ cup dark chocolate, chips or chopped, melted

DIRECTIONS

1. In a large saucepan, combine the butter, cream, chocolate-hazelnut spread, and coconut extract. Heat over medium heat until the mixture is melted.

2. Stir in the cocoa powder, sliced almonds, shredded coconut, oats, and salt.

3. Using a cookie scoop, shape the dough into 2-inch mounds and place on parchment paper, pressing firmly to smooth. The mixture may be soft.

4. Press a whole almond onto the top of each cookie.

5. Drizzle the melted dark chocolate over the top of each cookie.

6. Let the cookies sit for 2 to 3 hours at room temperature before serving.

Lemon Coconut Cookies

Yield: 24 cookies | Prep Time: 20 minutes | Cook Time: 8–10 minutes

With a cookie recipe this light and airy, it's no wonder they're called "clouds"! This lemon-coconut combination is always such a hit at parties, it's a surprise everyone isn't making them.

INGREDIENTS

1 (18.25-ounce) box lemon cake mix

1½ cups frozen whipped topping, thawed

1 large egg

½ cup sweetened shredded coconut

1 teaspoon lemon juice

2 teaspoons lemon extract

Confectioners' sugar

DIRECTIONS

1. Preheat the oven to 350°F. Line two baking sheets with parchment paper.

2. In a large bowl, beat the cake mix, whipped topping, egg, shredded coconut, lemon juice, and lemon extract until well combined.

3. Place the confectioners' sugar in a small bowl. Using a cookie scoop or your hands, shape the dough into 2-inch balls. (The dough will be very sticky. If using your hands, dust them lightly with the confectioners' sugar.) Roll the dough balls in the confectioners' sugar to coat. Place on the prepared baking sheets about 2 inches apart.

4. Bake for 8 to 10 minutes, until light brown.

5. Cool for 5 minutes, then transfer to a wire rack. Serve.

Tropical Paradise Cookies

Yield: 24 cookies | Prep Time: 10 minutes | Cook Time: 12–15 minutes

There's something about the drudgery of a rainy day that makes me start daydreaming of tropical locations. While I may be nowhere near a palm tree when I'm zipping up my raincoat, I can at least pretend that paradise is around the corner with these tropical treats.

INGREDIENTS

2 cups all-purpose flour

1½ teaspoons baking powder

½ teaspoon salt

¼ teaspoon baking soda

½ cup (1 stick) unsalted butter, softened

1 cup packed light brown sugar

1 (8-ounce) can pineapple chunks, drained

1 large egg

1 teaspoon vanilla extract

1 teaspoon orange zest (optional)

1½ cups shredded coconut

½ cup coarsely chopped macadamia nuts

Lime zest (optional)

DIRECTIONS

1. Preheat the oven to 350° F. Line two baking sheets with parchment paper.

2. In a medium bowl, combine the flour, baking powder, salt, and baking soda and toss well with a fork.

3. In a stand mixer fitted with the paddle attachment, beat the butter on medium-high speed for 2 minutes. Add the brown sugar and beat for an additional 2 minutes.

4. In a small bowl, combine the pineapple, egg, vanilla, and orange zest, if using. Add the pineapple mixture to the butter-sugar mixture and beat for 1 minute. With the mixer running on medium speed, gradually add the flour mixture. Stir in the shredded coconut and macadamia nuts by hand.

5. Using a cookie scoop, shape the dough into 1-inch balls and place on the prepared baking sheets about 2 inches apart. Bake for 12 to 15 minutes, until lightly browned.

6. Cool on wire racks. Top with lime zest (optional) and serve.

Cream Cheese Strawberry Cookies

Yield: 24 cookies | Prep Time: 20 minutes | Cook Time: 14–15 minutes

The key to making this dessert simply irresistible lies in the fresh strawberries and in soaking them in sweet fresh juice. This process is called macerating, and it brings out the natural sweetness in the fruit. They add that extra pop of flavor that reminds everyone of summer sunshine.

INGREDIENTS

¾ cup coarsely chopped fresh strawberries

2 tablespoons orange juice

1¼ cups plus 1 tablespoon all-purpose flour

½ teaspoon baking powder

⅛ teaspoon salt

4 tablespoons (½ stick) unsalted butter, softened

¾ cup sugar

2 ounces cream cheese, softened

2 ounces mascarpone cheese, softened

1 large egg

1 teaspoon vanilla extract

1 teaspoon orange zest

5 ounces white chocolate, coarsely chopped

Sugar for dusting

DIRECTIONS

1. Preheat the oven to 350°F. Line two baking sheets with parchment paper.

2. In a medium bowl, soak the strawberries in the orange juice for 2 to 3 minutes. Drain and set aside.

3. In another medium bowl, combine 1¼ cups flour, the baking powder, and salt.

4. In a large bowl, beat the butter, sugar, cream cheese, and mascarpone cheese using a hand mixer on medium-high speed until light and smooth. Add the egg, vanilla, and orange zest.

5. Slowly add the flour mixture to the cheese mixture until well combined. Stir in the white chocolate.

6. Sprinkle the strawberries with the remaining 1 tablespoon of flour and gently toss. Gently fold them into the batter.

7. Using a cookie scoop, shape the dough into 1-inch balls and place on the prepared baking sheets about 1 inch apart. Sprinkle with sugar.

8. Chill the cookies in the refrigerator for 5 to 10 minutes.

9. Bake for 14 to 15 minutes.

10. Cool for 2 to 3 minutes, then transfer to a wire rack to cool completely. Serve.

Crazy Good Cranberry Orange Cookies

Yield: 36 cookies | Prep Time: 15 minutes | Cook Time: 12–14 minutes

If you're looking for a festive dessert, then these cookies have your name written all over them. The cranberry-orange combination is perfect for the holiday season. They're going to be snapped up in a hurry!

INGREDIENTS

1 cup (2 sticks) unsalted butter, softened

1 cup granulated sugar

½ cup packed light brown sugar

1 large egg

1 teaspoon vanilla extract

1 teaspoon orange zest

2 tablespoons orange juice

2½ cups all-purpose flour

½ teaspoon baking soda

½ teaspoon salt

1½ cups fresh cranberries, halved

½ cup chopped hazelnuts

DIRECTIONS

1. Preheat the oven to 375°F. Line two baking sheets with parchment paper.

2. In a large bowl, cream the butter, granulated sugar, and brown sugar with a hand mixer on medium-high speed until smooth. Add the egg and vanilla and mix well.

3. Mix in the orange zest and orange juice.

4. In a large bowl, combine the flour, baking soda, and salt, then fold the flour mixture into the orange mixture.

5. Stir in the cranberries and hazelnuts.

6. Using a cookie scoop, shape the dough into 1-inch balls and place on the prepared baking sheets about 2 inches apart.

7. Bake for 12 to 14 minutes

8. Cool on wire racks.

Banana Bread Bites

Yield: 48 cookies | Prep Time: 20 minutes | Cook Time: 12–14 minutes

I could probably eat most of a loaf of banana bread in one sitting. It's so addicting that it's easy to convince yourself to have one more tiny slice. When you're feeling too lazy to bake a whole loaf of bread, turn to these cookies for the same satisfying snack in bite-size form.

INGREDIENTS

½ cup granulated sugar

½ cup packed light brown sugar

½ cup (1 stick) unsalted butter, softened

2 large eggs

1 cup mashed ripe bananas

1 teaspoon vanilla extract

2 cups all-purpose flour

1 teaspoon baking soda

½ teaspoon ground cinnamon

¼ teaspoon salt

1 cup semisweet chocolate chunks

½ cup chopped pecans

DIRECTIONS

1. Preheat the oven to 350°F. Line two baking sheets with parchment paper.

2. In a large bowl, combine the granulated sugar, brown sugar, and butter. Cream with a hand mixer on medium-high speed until light and fluffy. Add the eggs and mix well. Beat in the bananas and vanilla.

3. Slowly blend in the flour, baking soda, cinnamon, and salt.

4. Stir in the semisweet chocolate chunks and chopped pecans by hand.

5. Using a cookie scoop, shape the dough into 1-inch balls and place on the prepared baking sheets about 2 inches apart.

6. Bake for 12 to 14 minutes or until golden brown.

7. Cool on wire racks. Serve.

Butter Pecan Cake Mix Squares

Yield: 15 squares | Prep Time: 15 minutes | Cook Time: 40–45 minutes

Butter pecan was always the classy choice as far as ice cream flavors were concerned. It wasn't drowning in four kinds of chocolate and didn't need to be fancied up with syrups and sprinkles. These cookies embody that simple elegance.

INGREDIENTS

2 cups pecan halves

1 (15.25-ounce) box yellow butter–flavored cake mix

4 large eggs

½ cup (1 stick) unsalted butter, softened

8 ounces cream cheese, softened

3½ cups confectioners' sugar

½ cup store-bought butterscotch ice cream topping

DIRECTIONS

1. Preheat the oven to 350°F. Lightly coat a 9 × 13-inch baking dish with cooking spray.

2. Remove 15 perfect pecan halves and set them aside. Put the remaining pecans in a food processor and pulse to coarsely chop. Set aside.

3. In the same food processor bowl, combine the cake mix, 2 of the eggs, and the butter and pulse until blended. Stir in the chopped pecans with a spoon. Spread the batter in the prepared baking dish, pressing it into the corners and just slightly up the sides, about ½ inch.

4. In the same food processor bowl (no need to wash), combine the cream cheese, 2 remaining eggs, and the confectioners' sugar and process until smooth. Spread the cream cheese mixture over the bottom layer in the baking dish.

5. Bake for 40 to 45 minutes, until the top is set and golden brown.

6. Transfer the baking dish to a wire rack and cool for 2 to 3 minutes. Drizzle the butterscotch ice cream topping over the cookies in a diagonal pattern. Cool completely before cutting into bars. Place one pecan half in the center of each bar before serving.

Blueberry Muffin Cookies

Yield: 12–15 cookies | Prep Time: 10 minutes | Cook Time: 8–10 minutes

Whenever I see a freshly baked muffin at the bakery or coffee shop, I'm always tempted to buy it, just to enjoy that fluffy muffin top. I love these cookies because they take advantage of the best part of the muffin (that soft, billowy top) and are topped with a sweet citrus glaze.

INGREDIENTS

Cookies

1 (16.9-ounce) box blueberry muffin mix (Discard any topping mix. Separate the dried blueberries from the mix and rinse the blueberries.)

¾ cup old-fashioned oats

⅓ cup vegetable oil

¼ cup packed light brown sugar

½ teaspoon vanilla extract

¼ teaspoon salt

1 large egg, beaten

2 tablespoons half-and-half

Glaze

1½ cups confectioners' sugar

2 tablespoons unsalted butter, melted

2 teaspoons lemon juice

1 tablespoon half-and-half

Lemon zest for garnish

DIRECTIONS

1. Preheat the oven to 375°F. Line two baking sheets with parchment paper. Set aside.

2. In a large bowl, combine the muffin mix, oats, vegetable oil, brown sugar, vanilla, salt, egg, and half-and-half and stir together until a soft dough forms. Do not overmix. Gently fold the blueberries into the dough to combine.

3. Form the dough into 12 to 15 even piles on the prepared baking sheets. Bake for 8 to 10 minutes, rotating the pans halfway through baking. Remove from the oven and let them cool on the sheets.

4. Before serving, combine the confectioners' sugar, butter, and lemon juice in a small bowl. Stir to combine and add the half-and-half very slowly until the mixture reaches your desired consistency. Drizzle over the tops of the cookies and sprinkle with lemon zest.

4

Sugar and Spice

Sugar and spice truly do make everything nice.
Whether you're looking for an easy sugar cookie to
decorate for a baby shower or a simple spice recipe to
add more cheer to the holidays, these recipes show you
that old-fashioned recipes never go out of style.

Home-Style Amish Sugar Cookies

Yield: 24–30 cookies | Prep Time: 20 minutes | Cook Time: 10 minutes

Baking cookies from scratch can be an incredible stress reliever. This dough is so simple and easy to manipulate. Add a dash of milk if too dry or a tad more flour if too wet. Roll out and even cut with cute cutters. You won't be taking any shortcuts with this recipe, but believe me, the end result is worth the effort!

INGREDIENTS

2⅓ cups all-purpose flour

½ teaspoon baking soda

½ teaspoon baking powder

½ teaspoon cream of tartar

½ teaspoon salt

½ cup (1 stick) unsalted butter, softened

½ cup vegetable oil

½ cup granulated sugar

½ cup confectioners' sugar

1 large egg

1 teaspoon vanilla extract

¼ teaspoon lemon extract

Sprinkles or sanding sugar

DIRECTIONS

1. Preheat the oven to 375°F. Line two baking sheets with parchment paper.

2. In a large bowl, whisk together the flour, baking soda, baking powder, cream of tartar, and salt.

3. In a stand mixer fitted with the paddle attachment, cream the butter, vegetable oil, granulated sugar, and confectioners' sugar on medium-high until well combined. Add the egg, vanilla, and lemon extract and beat until well combined. Slowly add the flour mixture and mix until well combined.

4. Using a cookie scoop, shape the dough into 1-inch balls and place on the prepared baking sheets 2 inches apart. Flatten slightly using the bottom of a glass and top with sprinkles.

5. Bake for 10 minutes.

6. Cool on the baking sheets for a few minutes, then transfer to a wire rack to cool completely. Serve.

Bite-Size Cinnamon Roll Cookies

Yield: 48 cookies | Prep Time: 15 minutes plus 1 hour chilling time | Cook Time: 10 minutes

There's nothing like waking up to the smell of cinnamon rolls baking in the oven. Now you can re-create that magic anytime with these mouthwatering cinnamon roll cookies.

INGREDIENTS

Dough

2 teaspoons vanilla extract

1 teaspoon dry yeast

3¾ cups all-purpose flour, plus extra for flouring a work surface

½ teaspoon salt

1 cup granulated sugar

1½ cups (3 sticks) unsalted butter, softened

4 ounces cream cheese

Filling

½ cup packed light brown sugar

2 tablespoons ground cinnamon

½ cup dried dates, finely chopped

Frosting

1 cup confectioners' sugar

2–3 tablespoons whole milk

½ teaspoon ground cinnamon

½ teaspoon vanilla extract

DIRECTIONS

1. *For the dough:* In a small bowl, combine the vanilla and yeast. Stir to dissolve the yeast. Set aside.

2. In a large bowl, combine the flour, salt, and granulated sugar and toss to mix.

3. In a stand mixer fitted with the paddle attachment, beat the butter and cream cheese on medium-high speed until smooth. With the mixer running, add the vanilla-yeast mixture, then add the flour mixture—the dough will be crumbly, like a pie crust.

4. Turn the dough out onto a floured work surface. Gather it together into a smooth mound, then pat it into a 5 × 7-inch rectangle. Wrap in plastic wrap and chill for 1 hour or up to 24 hours.

5. *For the filling:* When ready to bake, preheat the oven to 375°F. Line two baking sheets with parchment paper. In a small bowl, combine the brown sugar, cinnamon, and dates.

6. Roll out the dough into a ¼-inch-thick rectangle. Spread the brown sugar mixture on top to within ½ inch on three sides, leaving a 1-inch border on one long edge. Roll the dough into a log toward the wider border. Cut the log crosswise into ⅓-inch-wide slices and place 1 inch apart on the prepared baking sheets. Bake for 10 minutes. Cool on the baking sheets set on wire racks.

7. *For the frosting:* While the cookies are cooling, in a medium bowl, combine the confectioners' sugar, milk, cinnamon, and vanilla until smooth.

8. Drizzle frosting on top and allow to cool and set completely. Serve.

Spice Bars

Yield: 24 bars | Prep Time: 20 minutes | Cook Time: 15–18 minutes

Are you ready to raid your spice cabinet for this one? These from-scratch spice bars are absolutely packed with flavor and put those forgotten spices to good use.

INGREDIENTS

⅓ cup vegetable oil

½ cup granulated sugar

½ cup packed light brown sugar

½ cup honey

2 cups all-purpose flour

1½ teaspoons ground cinnamon

¼ teaspoon ground ginger

¼ teaspoon ground cloves

1 teaspoon baking soda

½ teaspoon salt

2 large eggs, beaten

½ cup chopped pecans

½ cup golden raisins

DIRECTIONS

1. Preheat the oven to 350°F. Lightly coat a 9 × 13-inch baking dish with cooking spray.

2. In a large bowl, combine the vegetable oil, granulated sugar, brown sugar, and honey.

3. Add the flour, cinnamon, ginger, cloves, baking soda, and salt and mix well.

4. Add the eggs, pecans, and raisins and mix well.

5. Press the mixture evenly into the prepared baking dish. Bake for 15 to 18 minutes, until set. Cut into squares and serve.

Buttery Sugar Cookies

Yield: 48 cookies | Prep Time: 10 minutes plus 2 hours chilling time | Cook Time: 8–10 minutes

The hunt for the perfect sugar cookie is over. By including butter, we've added some creamy flavor to an old-school classic, allowing them to truly shine, and if you're looking for a great cutout cookie, look no further.

INGREDIENTS

½ cup granulated sugar

½ cup (1 stick) unsalted butter

½ cup butter-flavored vegetable shortening

1 teaspoon vanilla extract

½ teaspoon salt

1 large egg

2¼ cups cake flour, plus extra for flouring a work surface

¼–½ cup Demerara sugar, sugar sprinkles, or ground nuts

DIRECTIONS

1. In a stand mixer fitted with the paddle attachment, cream the granulated sugar, butter, and shortening on medium-high speed for 3 minutes, until very light and fluffy. Add the vanilla, salt, and egg and mix well. Gradually add the cake flour, scraping down the bowl once or twice, and mix to make a stiff dough.

2. On a floured work surface, form the dough into two logs 1½ inches in diameter, rolling them firmly into a perfectly round shape. Wrap the logs in plastic wrap or waxed paper and chill for 2 hours or up to 1 week.

3. When ready to bake, preheat the oven to 375°F. Line two baking sheets with parchment paper.

4. Cut the logs crosswise into ¼-inch-thick slices and place 1½ inches apart on the prepared baking sheets. Bake for 8 to 10 minutes, until the cookies are firm and the bottoms are a light golden brown. Sprinkle with the Demerara sugar, sugar sprinkles, or ground nuts.

5. Cool on the baking sheets set on wire racks for 2 minutes, then transfer the cookies to the racks to cool completely.

6. Store the cookies in an airtight container at room temperature for up to 5 days until ready to serve.

Snickerdoodles

Yield: 24 cookies | Prep Time: 20 minutes | Cook Time: 7 minutes

Who can resist the cinnamon goodness that is the famed snickerdoodle cookie? I love munching on these alongside a tall glass of milk while I'm buzzing away on my computer late at night. They make the perfect pick-me-up.

INGREDIENTS

½ cup (1 stick) unsalted butter, softened

½ cup vegetable shortening

1¾ cups sugar

2 large eggs

1 teaspoon vanilla extract

1¾ cups all-purpose flour

1 teaspoon baking soda

2 teaspoons cream of tartar

¼ teaspoon salt

4 teaspoons ground cinnamon

DIRECTIONS

1. Preheat the oven to 400°F. Line two baking sheets with parchment paper.

2. In a large bowl, cream together the unsalted butter, shortening, and 1½ cups of the sugar. Add the eggs and vanilla extract, and mix until well combined.

3. In a separate medium bowl, whisk together the flour, baking soda, cream of tartar, and salt. Gradually add to the butter mixture. Mix until combined, being careful not to overmix.

4. In a pie plate, mix together the remaining ¼ cup sugar and the ground cinnamon.

5. Using a cookie scoop, shape the dough into 1½-inch balls. Roll each in the cinnamon-sugar mixture and place on the prepared baking sheets about 2 inches apart. Bake for 7 minutes.

6. Cool on the baking sheets for 2 minutes, then transfer to a wire rack to cool completely before serving.

Ginger Snaps

Yield: 36 cookies | Prep Time: 15 minutes plus 1 hour chilling time | Cook Time: 10–12 minutes

It seems like every parent and grandparent has their own ginger snap recipe, ready to whip out at a moment's notice. This classic cookie is a hit all these years later for good reason—they're just too yummy to pass up, proving, once again, that classics never go out of style. The reason I love ginger snaps is their name—they truly snap when you bite into them!

INGREDIENTS

2¼ cups all-purpose flour

1 teaspoon baking soda

1½ teaspoons ground ginger

1 teaspoon ground cinnamon

¼ teaspoon salt

1 cup packed light brown sugar

¾ cup (1½ sticks) unsalted butter, softened

¼ cup molasses

1 large egg

¼ cup granulated sugar, plus extra for topping

DIRECTIONS

1. In a large bowl, whisk together 1 cup of the flour, the baking soda, ginger, cinnamon, and salt. Mix in the brown sugar.

2. In a small microwave-safe bowl, melt the butter in the microwave. Mix the melted butter into the flour mixture. Add the molasses and egg and mix until well combined.

3. Switch to a heavy wooden spoon and stir in the remaining 1¼ cups flour until well combined. Cover the bowl with plastic wrap and chill for 1 hour or up to overnight.

4. Preheat the oven to 350°F with a rack in the center position. Line two baking sheets with parchment paper.

5. Put the granulated sugar in a small bowl. Using a cookie scoop, shape the dough into 1-inch balls. Roll the balls in the granulated sugar to coat. Place the balls on the prepared baking sheets about 2 inches apart. Sprinkle with sugar.

6. Bake for 10 to 12 minutes. The cookies will flatten after puffing slightly.

7. Cool on the baking sheets for 2 minutes, sprinkle with additional sugar, then transfer to wire racks to cool completely. Serve.

Soda Pop Cookies

Yield: 24 cookies | Prep Time: 10 minutes | Cook Time: 10–13 minutes

Soda pop not only adds moisture to a cookie but also helps the cookie achieve the perfect balance of fluffiness and flavor. I used root beer with these particular cookies, but feel free to substitute with your favorite type.

INGREDIENTS

Cookies

2½ cups all-purpose flour

½ teaspoon salt

½ teaspoon baking soda

½ teaspoon baking powder

8 tablespoons unsalted butter, softened

¾ cup granulated sugar

½ cup packed light brown sugar

2 teaspoons vanilla extract

1 large egg, room temperature

½ cup soda pop

Frosting

8 tablespoons unsalted butter, softened

4 cups confectioners' sugar

⅓ cup soda pop

DIRECTIONS

1. *For the cookies:* Preheat the oven to 350°F. Line two baking sheets with parchment paper. Set aside.

2. In a large bowl, combine the flour, salt, baking soda, and baking powder.

3. In another bowl, cream together the butter, granulated sugar, brown sugar, and vanilla until light and fluffy. Add in the egg, then the soda pop, and mix until just combined.

4. Slowly add the flour mixture, about one cup at a time, until just combined.

5. Scoop in 1½ tablespoon portions onto prepared baking sheets and space the cookies about 2 inches apart.

6. Bake for 10 to 13 minutes. Remove from the oven and allow the cookies to cool for about 3 minutes. Then transfer to a cooling rack to cool completely.

7. *For the frosting:* Beat the butter with 1 cup of the confectioners' sugar until it begins to turn creamy. Once it's smooth and light in color, add the soda pop. Then add in the remaining 3 cups of confectioners' sugar, one cup at a time. Frost the cooled cookies and serve.

Danish Spice Cookies

Yield: 36 cookies | Prep Time: 5 minutes plus 1 hour chilling time | Cook Time: 10–11 minutes

Otherwise known as *speculoos*, these cookies are the ones I look forward to the most each holiday season. The special blend of spices used to make these beauties smells like the essence of the holidays. Presses used to make traditional designs are available online at retailers like Fancy Flours or Fante's Kitchen Shop, but you can simply press the cookies flat with the bottom of a glass, if you'd like.

INGREDIENTS

½ cup (1 stick) unsalted butter, softened

½ cup granulated sugar

¾ cup packed light brown sugar

1 large egg

1½ teaspoons vanilla extract

¼ teaspoon baking soda

½ teaspoon salt

2½ teaspoons ground cinnamon

¾ teaspoon ground nutmeg

½ teaspoon ground ginger

¼ teaspoon ground cardamom

1¾ cups all-purpose flour

Cinnamon sugar for sprinkling

DIRECTIONS

1. In a large bowl using a hand mixer, cream the butter, granulated sugar, and brown sugar on medium-high speed until well combined. Add the egg and vanilla. Mix well. Add the baking soda, salt, cinnamon, nutmeg, ginger, cardamom, and flour. Mix well.

2. Refrigerate the dough for about 1 hour.

3. Preheat the oven to 375°F. Line two baking sheets with parchment paper.

4. Using a cookie scoop, shape the dough into 1-inch balls and place on the prepared baking sheets about 2 inches apart. Use a cookie press or the bottom of a glass to flatten each ball until they are about ¼ inch thick.

5. Sprinkle the tops of the cookies with cinnamon sugar. Bake for 10 to 11 minutes, until lightly golden brown around the edges.

6. Cool for 10 minutes before serving.

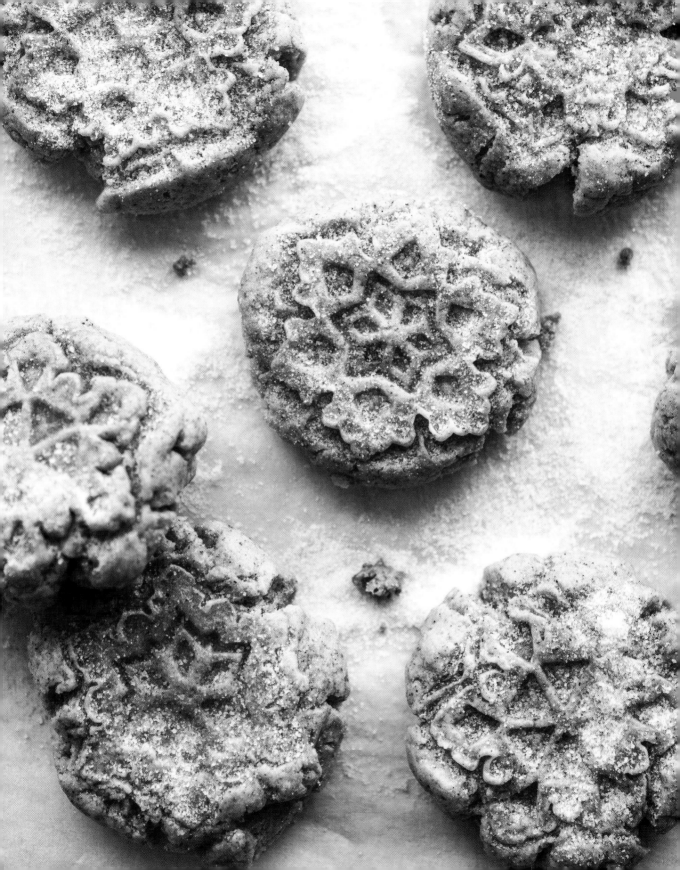

Linzer Cookies

Yield: 24 cookies | Prep Time: 25 minutes plus 30 minutes chilling time | Cook Time: 8–10 minutes

Feel free to mix and match jam flavors to create a more colorful spread! I like sticking with raspberry, since the deep red color looks so festive.

INGREDIENTS

½ cup vegetable shortening, softened

4 tablespoons (½ stick) unsalted butter, softened

¼ cup sour cream

½ cup granulated sugar

½ cup packed light brown sugar

1 large egg

1 teaspoon vanilla extract

2½ cups plus 2 tablespoons all-purpose flour

½ cup cornstarch

1 teaspoon baking powder

½ teaspoon salt

¾ cup seedless raspberry jam

¼ cup confectioners' sugar

DIRECTIONS

1. In a stand mixer fitted with the paddle attachment, combine the shortening, butter, and sour cream and beat on medium-high speed for 1 minute, until smooth. Add the granulated sugar and brown sugar and beat on medium speed for 2 minutes, until light and creamy, scraping down the bowl once. With the machine running, add the egg and vanilla.

2. In a large bowl, combine 2½ cups of the flour, the cornstarch, baking powder, and salt and toss with a fork to mix. With the mixer running, add the flour mixture gradually and beat just until all the dry ingredients are incorporated. Scrape down the bowl, transfer the dough to a work surface, and divide it in half. Form each half into an 8-inch disc and wrap in plastic wrap. Refrigerate for at least 30 minutes and up to overnight.

3. Preheat the oven to 350°F. Line two baking sheets with parchment paper.

4. Remove one disc of dough and roll it out on a lightly floured surface to ⅛-inch thickness. Cut using a 3-inch cookie cutter, placing the cutouts about 1 inch apart on the prepared baking sheets. Repeat with the second disc. Use a smaller cookie cutter to cut the centers from half the rounds.

5. Bake for 8 to 10 minutes, until the bottoms are just beginning to brown around the edges. Cool on wire racks.

6. Place the uncut cookies on a work surface and spread them evenly with a thin layer of the jam. Use a small sieve to sprinkle confectioners' sugar over the cookies with the cutouts, then gently place them on top of the jam-covered cookies and press very lightly to adhere. Serve.

Maple Sugar Cookies

Yield: 24 cookies | Prep Time: 15–20 minutes | Cook Time: 15–18 minutes

It's always such a treat to chow down on maple sugar candy, but you don't have to wait for fall anymore. These maple sugar cookies give you all the flavor you're looking for in just one bite. (Plus, they make excellent cookie sandwiches!)

INGREDIENTS

Cookies

2½ cups all-purpose flour

¾ teaspoon baking soda

1 teaspoon baking powder

¼ teaspoon kosher salt

1 cup (2 sticks) unsalted butter, softened

1½ cups granulated sugar

3 egg yolks

1 teaspoon vanilla extract

2 tablespoons maple syrup

Maple Icing

4 tablespoons (½ stick) unsalted butter, melted

¼ cup heavy cream

3 tablespoons maple syrup

3–3½ cups confectioners' sugar

DIRECTIONS

1. *For the cookies:* Preheat the oven to 350°F. Line two baking sheets with parchment paper.

2. In a large bowl, combine the flour, baking soda, baking powder, and salt.

3. In a stand mixer fitted with the paddle attachment, cream the butter and 1¼ cups of the granulated sugar on medium-high speed until combined. Add the egg yolks, vanilla, and maple syrup. Slowly add the flour mixture and mix just until combined.

4. Put the remaining ¼ cup granulated sugar in a small bowl. Using a cookie scoop, shape the dough into 2-inch balls, then roll them in the sugar to coat. Place on the prepared baking sheets about 2 inches apart.

5. Bake for 15 to 18 minutes, until the tops of the cookies start to crack.

6. Cool on the baking sheets for 5 minutes, then transfer to a wire rack to cool completely.

7. *For the maple icing:* In a medium bowl, combine the melted butter, cream, and maple syrup. Slowly add the confectioners' sugar and mix until smooth.

8. Drizzle the icing over the cooled cookies and serve.

Salted Caramel Bites

Yield: 24 cookies | Prep Time: 15–20 minutes | Cook Time: 10–12 minutes

These caramel bites are almost like having the essence of fall wrapped up in a snack-size dessert. The never-ending caramel flavor reminds me of fall fairs and Oktoberfest, and the salty twist at the end will keep you grabbing for another.

INGREDIENTS

2½ cups all-purpose flour

¾ teaspoon baking soda

1 teaspoon baking powder

¼ teaspoon kosher salt

1 cup (2 sticks) unsalted butter, softened

1¼ cups granulated sugar

3 egg yolks

1 teaspoon vanilla extract

2 tablespoons maple syrup

Caramel sauce

2 tablespoons sea salt

DIRECTIONS

1. Preheat the oven to 350°F. Line two baking sheets with parchment paper.

2. In a large bowl, combine the flour, baking soda, baking powder, and salt.

3. In a stand mixer fitted with the paddle attachment, cream the softened butter and granulated sugar on medium speed until combined. Add the egg yolks, vanilla, and 2 tablespoons of the maple syrup. Slowly add the flour mixture and mix just until combined.

4. Using a cookie scoop, shape the dough into 1-inch balls and place on the prepared baking sheets about 2 inches apart.

5. Bake for 10 to 12 minutes, until the tops of the cookies start to crack.

6. Cool on the baking sheets for 5 minutes, then transfer to a wire rack to cool completely.

7. Slowly drizzle the caramel sauce over the cooled cookies and top with the sea salt before serving.

Buttery Thumbprints

Yield: 36 cookies | Prep Time: 20 minutes | Cook Time: 12–15 minutes

These colorful cookies really brighten up a dessert spread. I love picking out a few different jam flavors and colors to create a wide assortment to offer guests. It's so easy to present so many different varieties!

INGREDIENTS

2½ cups all-purpose flour, plus extra for flouring hands

1½ teaspoons baking powder

½ teaspoon ground nutmeg

¼ teaspoon ground cinnamon

Pinch of salt

1¼ cups sugar

¾ cup vegetable shortening, softened

½ cup buttermilk

2 large eggs

½ teaspoon baking soda

½ teaspoon vanilla extract

¼ cup jam or jelly of your choice

DIRECTIONS

1. Preheat the oven to 350°F. Line two baking sheets with parchment paper.

2. In a stand mixer fitted with the paddle attachment, combine 2½ cups of the flour, the baking powder, nutmeg, cinnamon, salt, and sugar. Stir briefly to mix well. Add the shortening and mix to form coarse crumbs.

3. In a small bowl or measuring cup, combine the buttermilk, eggs, baking soda, and vanilla. With the mixer running, gradually add the buttermilk mixture until a soft dough is formed.

4. Using a cookie scoop, shape the dough into 1-inch balls and roll in lightly floured palms to smooth. Place on the prepared baking sheets about 1½ inches apart. Use the back of a measuring spoon to make "thumbprint" depressions in each cookie and fill with ½ teaspoon of the jam or jelly.

5. Bake for 12 to 15 minutes.

6. Cool on the baking sheets for at least 5 minutes, then transfer to a wire rack to cool completely. Serve.

Grandma's Spice Cookies

Yield: 36 cookies | Prep Time: 15 minutes plus 1 hour chilling time | Cook Time: 12 minutes

Grandmothers always have the best-smelling kitchens. When you bake up these incredible spice cookies, they'll do more than just satisfy that sweet-tooth craving—they'll remind you of family.

INGREDIENTS

2 cups all-purpose flour

1 tablespoon ground ginger

2 teaspoons baking soda

2 teaspoons ground cinnamon, divided

½ teaspoon salt

⅓ cup chopped candied ginger (2 ounces)

1 cup packed light brown sugar

¾ cup butter-flavored vegetable shortening, at room temperature

1 large egg

¼ cup molasses

¼ cup granulated sugar

DIRECTIONS

1. Preheat the oven to 350°F. Line two baking sheets with parchment paper.

2. In a medium bowl, combine the flour, ground ginger, baking soda, 1 teaspoon of the cinnamon, and salt. Add the candied ginger and toss with a fork to mix.

3. In a stand mixer fitted with the paddle attachment, beat the brown sugar and vegetable shortening on medium-high speed for 2 minutes, until light and fluffy. With the mixer running, add the egg and molasses, then gradually add the flour mixture, mixing only until all the dry ingredients are moistened.

4. Cover the bowl with plastic wrap and chill for 1 hour or up to 1 day.

5. In a small bowl, combine the granulated sugar and remaining 1 teaspoon cinnamon. Using a cookie scoop, shape the dough into 1-inch balls. Roll in the cinnamon-sugar and place on baking sheets 2 inches apart.

6. Bake for 12 minutes until lightly browned, then transfer to wire racks to cool completely. The cookies can be stored in an airtight container at room temperature for up to 1 week or frozen for up to 1 month.

5

Chocolate

I can understand if you skipped over the first four chapters just to get straight to the chocolate. After all, there's no better way to get to someone's heart, right? These chocolaty treats really can lift you up on days when you're feeling a bit blue, which is why you always need to have a few handy! From classy Mint Chocolate Cookies (page 144) to serve to guests to our kid-friendly Gooey Turtle Bars (page 135) that'll have you restocking your napkins, there's something here for everyone.

The Best Chocolate Chip Cookies Ever

Yield: 48 cookies | Prep Time: 15 minutes | Cook Time: 8 minutes

Everyone has their secret go-to cookie recipe, and I'm pleased to say this one's my specialty. It's extra buttery, which makes the dough super creamy and makes the final product richer than ever!

INGREDIENTS

1½ cups packed light brown sugar

1½ cups granulated sugar

1 cup (2 sticks) unsalted butter, softened

½ cup butter-flavored vegetable shortening, softened

4 large eggs

2 teaspoons vanilla extract

2 teaspoons salt

2 teaspoons baking soda

5 cups all-purpose flour

1 (24-ounce) bag semisweet chocolate chips

DIRECTIONS

1. Preheat the oven to 350°F. Line two baking sheets with parchment paper.

2. In a stand mixer fitted with the paddle attachment, cream the brown sugar, granulated sugar, butter, and shortening on medium speed until pale. Add the eggs, one at a time, scraping down the sides of the bowl after each addition. Add the vanilla, salt, and baking soda.

3. Add the flour, 1 cup at a time, mixing until each cup is well combined before adding the next. Add the chocolate chips.

4. Using a cookie scoop, shape the dough into 1-inch balls and place on the prepared baking sheets about 2 inches apart.

5. Bake for 8 minutes.

6. Cool for 10 minutes before serving.

Alex's Cowboy Cookies

Yield: 30 cookies | Prep Time: 15 minutes | Cook Time: 12–15 minutes

My husband has the biggest sweet tooth I know. There isn't a night that goes by that I don't see him chowing down on something sugary before bed. These cowboy cookies are his absolute favorite. I know if I make a batch of these, they'll be gone in a couple of days!

INGREDIENTS

2 cups all-purpose flour

1 teaspoon baking soda

½ teaspoon baking powder

½ teaspoon salt

2 cups old-fashioned rolled oats

¾ cup (1½ sticks) unsalted butter, softened

1¼ cups granulated sugar

1 cup packed light brown sugar

2 large eggs

1 teaspoon vanilla extract

½ cup raisins

½ cup raw pecan pieces

½ cup sweetened shredded coconut

½ cup semisweet chocolate chips

DIRECTIONS

1. Preheat the oven to 350°F. Line two baking sheets with parchment paper.

2. In a medium bowl, combine the flour, baking soda, baking powder, salt, and oats and toss with a fork to mix.

3. In a stand mixer fitted with the paddle attachment, beat the butter, 1 cup of the granulated sugar, and the brown sugar on medium-high speed for 2 minutes, until creamy. With the machine running on medium speed, add the eggs and vanilla and beat for an additional 2 minutes. By hand, fold in the raisins, pecans, coconut, and chocolate chips—the batter will be stiff and thick.

4. Put the remaining ¼ cup granulated sugar in a small bowl. Using a cookie scoop, shape the dough into 2-inch balls, then roll each in your palms to smooth the outside. Dip the ball into the sugar and place on the prepared baking sheets about 1½ inches apart. Use the bottom of a glass to gently press each into a 1½-inch circle.

5. Bake for 12 to 15 minutes until the cookies are firm.

6. Cool on wire racks. These cookies hold very well and will keep in an airtight container at room temperature for up to 1 week or in the freezer for up to 6 months.

Chocolate Haystacks

Yield: 24–36 cookies | Prep Time: 15 minutes | Cook Time: 1 hour chilling time

I love to make this no-bake recipe during the summer when it's hot and humid outside. The last thing you want to do is turn on your oven! The kids will love helping you break up the chow mein noodles, which give the cookies extra crunch.

INGREDIENTS

1 cup dark chocolate chips

1 cup peanut butter chips

1 tablespoon vegetable shortening

1 (6-ounce) package chow mein noodles, coarsely broken

½ cup chopped cashews

Sea salt

DIRECTIONS

1. In a medium microwave-safe bowl, combine the dark chocolate chips, peanut butter chips, and shortening and microwave for 1 minute on high power. Stir and continue to microwave in 15-second intervals, stirring after each, until melted.

2. Stir in the chow mein noodles and cashews until well combined.

3. Line two baking sheets with parchment paper.

4. Using a cookie scoop, shape the dough into 1-inch balls and place on the prepared baking sheets about 2 inches apart. Sprinkle the tops with sea salt.

5. Chill for 1 hour, until set. Serve.

Chewy Brownie Cookies

Yield: 24 cookies | Prep Time: 20 minutes | Cook Time: 10 minutes

Brownies are a timeless favorite, so why not put that same moist chocolaty goodness in a cookie, too? Now you don't have to choose between them!

INGREDIENTS

4 (4-ounce) 70 to 75% cacao dark chocolate baking bars

3 tablespoons unsalted butter

¼ cup all-purpose flour

¼ teaspoon baking powder

2 large eggs

⅔ cup sugar

1 teaspoon vanilla extract

½ teaspoon salt

½ cup chopped walnuts

DIRECTIONS

1. Fill a saucepan with 1 inch of water and bring the water to a simmer. Finely chop 3 of the bars of dark chocolate and place in a heatproof glass bowl with the unsalted butter. Set the bowl over the simmering water (be sure the bottom of the bowl does not touch the water) and heat over low heat until melted.

2. Chop the remaining chocolate bar into ¼-to ½-inch chunks and set aside.

3. In a small bowl, sift together the flour and baking powder and set aside.

4. While the chocolate is melting, in a stand mixer fitted with the paddle attachment, combine the eggs, sugar, vanilla, and salt and beat on medium-high speed for 10 minutes—the mixture will become light and fluffy and double in volume. Turn the mixer speed down to medium and add the flour mixture, scraping down the bowl, and mix until well combined. Stir in the chopped chocolate and walnuts by hand. Cover the bowl and let stand at room temperature for 1 hour.

5. Preheat the oven to 350°F. Line two baking sheets with parchment paper.

6. Using a cookie scoop, shape the dough into 2-inch balls and place on the prepared baking sheets 2 inches about apart. Bake for about 10 minutes, until cookies are slightly firm in the center.

7. Cool completely on wire racks. The cookies can be stored in an airtight container, separated by sheets of waxed paper, at room temperature for up to 5 days.

Gooey Turtle Bars

Yield: 24 bars | Prep Time: 20 minutes | Cook Time: 30 minutes

This might just be the gooiest dessert in the bunch! With a combination of chocolate chips, caramel topping, and pecans, you're going to have the neighbors practically begging you for the recipe.

INGREDIENTS

1 (16.5-ounce) roll refrigerated sugar cookie dough

2 cups semisweet chocolate chips

3 cups chopped pecans

½ cup (1 stick) unsalted butter

½ cup packed light brown sugar

1 (12.25-ounce) jar caramel ice cream topping

DIRECTIONS

1. Preheat the oven to 350°F. Line a 9 × 13-inch baking dish with parchment paper, with 2 inches of overhang on each long side of the pan.

2. Use your fingertips to press the refrigerated sugar cookie dough into the pan in an even layer.

3. Sprinkle half the semisweet chocolate chips and pecans over the dough.

4. In a small saucepan, melt the butter over low heat, then stir in the brown sugar and caramel ice cream topping. Raise the heat slightly and bring to a boil, stirring frequently. Evenly pour over the chocolate chips and pecans layer. Top with the remaining chocolate chips and pecans.

5. Bake until the edges are deep brown, about 30 minutes. The topping will be very runny but will set up as it cools.

6. Cool on a wire rack for several hours or overnight before using the edges of the parchment paper to remove the entire layer from the pan for easier cutting.

Incredible Buckeye Brownie Cookies

Yield: 24 cookies | Prep Time: 30 minutes | Cook Time: 10 minutes

I love making a batch of buckeye cookies to bring along when tailgating before a football game. The Midwesterner in me can't resist a subtle "Buckeye" reference. The creamy peanut butter center never fails to get everyone talking because it's such a welcome surprise!

INGREDIENTS

8 ounces bittersweet chocolate, chopped

2 tablespoons unsalted butter, softened

2 large eggs

½ teaspoon vanilla extract

½ cup plus 2 tablespoons granulated sugar

½ cup all-purpose flour

¼ teaspoon baking powder

¼ teaspoon instant espresso powder

1 cup semisweet chocolate chips

1 cup creamy peanut butter

1 cup confectioners' sugar

DIRECTIONS

1. Preheat the oven to 350°F. Line two baking sheets with parchment paper.

2. In a small microwave-safe bowl, combine the bittersweet chocolate and butter and microwave in 30-second intervals, stirring after each, until melted.

3. In a large bowl, stir together the eggs, vanilla, and ½ cup of the granulated sugar. In another large bowl, whisk together the flour, baking powder, and espresso powder.

4. Add the melted chocolate to the egg mixture. Slowly add the flour mixture.

5. Add the semisweet chocolate chips to the batter. Chill the dough for 20 to 30 minutes.

6. In a medium bowl, combine the peanut butter and confectioners' sugar. Using your hands, shape into 1-inch balls and set aside.

7. Using a cookie scoop, shape the dough into 2-inch balls and place on the prepared baking sheets about 2 inches apart. Bake for 10 minutes, until they start to set up. Do not overbake.

8. Remove the cookies from the oven. While the cookies are still warm, press one peanut butter ball into the center of each cookie, allowing them to flatten and spread without hitting the edges.

9. Cool for 5 minutes, then transfer to a wire rack to cool completely. Serve.

5-Minute No-Bake Cookies

Yield: 24 cookies | Prep Time: 15–20 minutes | Cook Time: 1 minute

You don't need to spend hours in the kitchen to turn out a tasty dessert. These no-bake cookies take less than 5 minutes to cook, which gives you even more time to enjoy their creamy chocolaty goodness.

INGREDIENTS

½ cup (1 stick) unsalted butter

2 cups sugar

¼ cup unsweetened cocoa powder

¼ teaspoon instant espresso powder

⅛ teaspoon sea salt

¼ cup heavy cream

¼ cup whole milk

2 teaspoons vanilla extract

¼ cup creamy peanut butter

¼ cup chocolate-hazelnut spread

3 cups quick-cooking oats

¼ cup chopped hazelnuts

DIRECTIONS

1. Line a baking sheet with parchment paper.

2. In a large saucepan, combine the butter, sugar, cocoa powder, espresso powder, salt, cream, and milk. Bring the mixture to a full boil, stirring occasionally. Boil for 30 to 45 seconds without stirring. Remove from the heat and set aside to cool for 2 to 3 minutes.

3. Add the vanilla, peanut butter, chocolate-hazelnut spread, oats, and hazelnuts and mix well.

4. Using a cookie scoop, shape the dough into 2-inch balls and place on the prepared baking sheet about 1 inch apart.

5. Allow to set before serving.

Cream Cheese Chocolate Chip Cookies

Yield: 30–40 cookies | Prep Time: 15 minutes, plus 2 hours chilling time | Cook Time: 8–10 minutes

Make-ahead desserts are my time-saving secret. All I have to do for this recipe is prep the dough ahead of time and pop it in the freezer, and then I can easily bake up a batch whenever I have the time. The combination of butter and cream cheese makes this dough super moist and freezable, so it's perfect for those weeks when you have a hectic schedule!

INGREDIENTS

2¼ cups all-purpose flour

2 teaspoons cornstarch

1 teaspoon baking soda

¼ teaspoon salt

½ cup (1 stick) unsalted butter, softened

2 ounces cream cheese, softened

¾ cup packed light brown sugar

¼ cup granulated sugar

1 large egg

2 teaspoons vanilla extract

1 (11.5-ounce) bag chocolate chunks

DIRECTIONS

1. Line two baking sheets with parchment paper.

2. In a medium bowl, combine the flour, cornstarch, baking soda, and salt and toss to mix well.

3. In a stand mixer fitted with the paddle attachment, combine the butter and cream cheese and beat on medium-high speed for 2 minutes. Add the brown sugar and granulated sugar and beat for an additional 2 minutes, until light and fluffy. Add the egg and vanilla, scrape down the bowl, and gradually add the flour mixture until well mixed. Stir in the chocolate chunks by hand.

4. Using a cookie scoop, shape the dough into 2-inch balls and place on the prepared baking sheets about 2 inches apart. Chill in the refrigerator for 2 hours or freeze.

5. When ready to bake, preheat the oven to 350°F. Bake the cookies from the refrigerator for 8 to 10 minutes or directly from the freezer for 12 minutes.

6. Cool on the baking sheets for 5 minutes, then transfer to wire racks to cool. Store in an airtight container at room temperature for up to 1 week.

Monster Cookies

Yield: 24 cookies | Prep Time: 20 minutes, plus 30 minutes chilling time | Cook Time: 10 minutes

If you can't quite decide what you're in the mood for, these Monster Cookies have you covered. With peanut butter, oats, M&M's, and chocolate chips, they're a dream dessert for the indecisive baker . . . or when you're looking to use up some leftover Halloween candy.

INGREDIENTS

½ cup (1 stick) unsalted butter, softened

½ cup light brown sugar, packed

¼ cup granulated sugar

1 large egg

¾ cup creamy peanut butter

1 teaspoon vanilla extract

¼ teaspoon salt

1¼ cups all-purpose flour

½ teaspoon baking soda

½ cup quick-cooking oats

¾ cup M&M's

½ cup semisweet chocolate chips

⅓ cup chocolate candy sprinkles

DIRECTIONS

1. Preheat the oven to 350°F. Line two baking sheets with parchment paper.

2. In a large bowl, cream together the butter, brown sugar, and granulated sugar. Add the egg, peanut butter, vanilla, and salt. Mix until well combined.

3. In a separate medium bowl, whisk together the flour and baking soda. Gradually add to the butter mixture. Mix until combined, being careful to not overmix. Fold in the oats, M&M's, chocolate chips, and chocolate candy sprinkles. Chill the dough for 30 minutes. Using a cookie scoop, shape the dough into 2-inch balls and place on the prepared baking sheets about 2 inches apart. Top with extra chocolate candy sprinkles.

4. Bake for 9 to 10 minutes.

5. Cool on the baking sheets for 10 minutes; the cookies will firm slightly as they cool. Serve.

Mint Chocolate Cookies

Yield: 36 cookies | Prep Time: 15–20 minutes | Cook Time: 8–10 minutes

There's something about mint that adds a little bit of sophistication to any dessert. I love offering these to my in-laws when they come to visit—I get rave reviews every time!

INGREDIENTS

2¾ cups all-purpose flour

1 teaspoon baking soda

½ teaspoon baking powder

½ teaspoon salt

1 cup (2 sticks) unsalted butter, softened

1½ cups granulated sugar

1 large egg

1 teaspoon mint extract

2½ ounces Andes mints, chopped

2½ ounces dark chocolate baking morsels with mint filling

DIRECTIONS

1. Preheat the oven to 375°F. Line two baking sheets with parchment paper.

2. In a large bowl, combine the flour, baking soda, baking powder, and salt.

3. In another large bowl, cream the unsalted butter and sugar using a hand mixer on medium-high speed until smooth. Beat in the egg and mint extract. Slowly add the flour mixture and beat until combined.

4. Fold in the Andes mints and chocolate-mint baking morsels by hand.

5. Using a cookie scoop, shape the dough into 1-inch balls and place on the prepared baking sheets about 2 inches apart. Flatten slightly with the bottom of a glass.

6. Bake for 8 to 10 minutes.

7. Cool for 2 minutes, then transfer to a wire rack to cool completely.

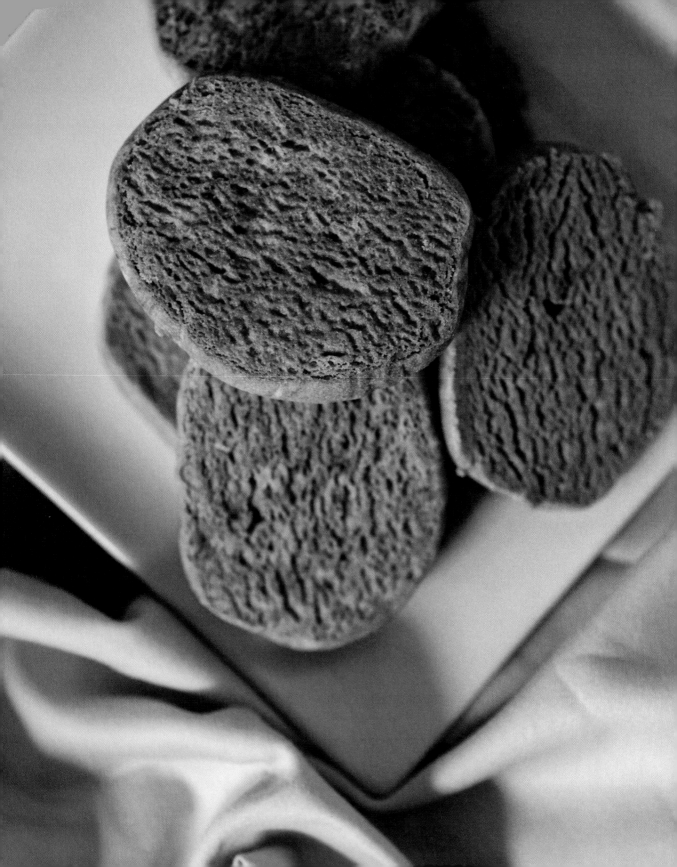

Chocolate Shortbread

Yield: 36 cookies | Prep Time: 15 minutes, plus 1 hour chilling time | Cook Time: 20–25 minutes

Shortbread cookies are super versatile. I love to stock up on different frostings, icings, and candies when I make these, so I can decorate them to my heart's content. Feel free to be creative or leave them as is for an understated treat.

INGREDIENTS

1 cup (2 sticks) unsalted butter, softened

¾ cup granulated sugar

1 teaspoon vanilla extract

2 cups all-purpose flour

¼ cup unsweetened cocoa powder

¼ teaspoon salt

DIRECTIONS

1. In a stand mixer fitted with the paddle attachment or in a large bowl using a hand mixer, beat the butter for about 5 minutes, until light and fluffy. Add the granulated sugar and mix until well combined and very light in color. Add the vanilla and mix well.

2. In another large bowl, whisk together the flour, cocoa powder, and salt. With the mixer running on low speed, gradually add the flour mixture, stopping as soon as all the flour has been incorporated. Do not overmix.

3. Form the dough into a log 2 inches in diameter, wrap it in plastic wrap, and refrigerate for 1 hour.

4. Preheat the oven to 325°F. Line two baking sheets with parchment paper.

5. Remove the dough from the fridge. Cut into ¼-inch slices and place on the prepared baking sheets about 2 inches apart. Bake until firm, 20 to 25 minutes. Be sure to rotate the baking sheets halfway through cooking.

6. Cool completely on a wire rack and serve.

Toasted S'mores Cookies

Yield: 16 large cookies | Prep Time: 30 minutes plus 2 hours chilling time | Cook Time: 12 minutes

I like to pull out this recipe when it's too cool outside to start a campfire, but I'm still craving that winning marshmallow-and-chocolate combination.

INGREDIENTS

Cookies

2¼ cups all-purpose flour

1 teaspoon baking soda

1½ teaspoons cornstarch

½ teaspoon kosher salt

¾ cup (1½ sticks) unsalted butter, melted

¾ cup packed light brown sugar

½ cup granulated sugar

1 large egg

1 egg yolk

2 teaspoons vanilla extract

1 cup semisweet chocolate chips

S'more Toppings

16 miniature milk chocolate bars

16 large marshmallows

DIRECTIONS

1. *For the cookies:* In a large bowl, combine the flour, baking soda, cornstarch, and salt.

2. In a medium bowl, whisk together the melted butter, brown sugar, and granulated sugar until well combined and smooth.

3. Mix the egg and egg yolk into the butter mixture, then add the vanilla.

4. Combine the wet and dry ingredients and mix well. Fold in the semisweet chocolate chips.

5. Cover the dough and chill for 2 hours or up to overnight.

6. Remove the dough from the refrigerator and let it soften at room temperature for about 15 minutes.

7. Preheat the oven to 325°F. Line two baking sheets with parchment paper.

8. Using a cookie scoop or your hands, shape the dough into 3-inch balls and place on the prepared baking sheets 2 to 3 inches apart.

9. Bake for 10 minutes.

10. *For the s'more toppings:* Remove the cookies from the oven. Gently place a chocolate bar on top, then press a marshmallow in the center of each.

11. Return to the oven for 2 minutes to melt the toppings.

12. Turn on the broiler to toast the topping, or use a kitchen torch.

13. Cool for 10 minutes on the baking sheets, then transfer to a wire rack to cool completely. Serve.

My-Goodness-These-Are-Amazing Cookies

Yield: 36 cookies | Prep Time: 20 minutes | Cook Time: 10 minutes

How can you go wrong with a chocolate-hazelnut spread recipe? When combined with smooth, creamy peanut butter and crunchy cereal, this dessert becomes heaven in a bite-size morsel.

INGREDIENTS

1 cup sugar

1 cup light corn syrup

1½ cups creamy peanut butter

1 cup chocolate-hazelnut spread

6 cups Special K Oats & Honey cereal

4 ounces semisweet or dark chocolate chunks

DIRECTIONS

1. In a medium saucepan, combine the sugar and corn syrup and cook on medium heat, stirring well, until boiling. Remove from the heat and stir in the peanut butter and chocolate-hazelnut spread.

2. Pour the cereal into a large bowl, then pour the peanut butter mixture over the cereal and combine well, covering all the cereal flakes.

3. Line a baking sheet with parchment paper. Using a cookie scoop, shape the dough into 2-inch balls and place on the prepared baking sheet about 2 inches apart.

4. Put the chocolate in a small microwave-safe bowl and microwave in 30-second intervals, stirring after each, until melted. Drizzle over the cookie balls. Serve.

Mocha Polka Dot Cookies

Yield: 36 cookies | Prep Time: 15 minutes | Cook Time: 12–15 minutes

Adding just the slightest bit of espresso powder packs a big punch, turning a simple cookie recipe into a standout favorite. I love serving these up during a weekend brunch as I refill everyone's mugs of coffee.

INGREDIENTS

2 cups all-purpose flour

3 tablespoons unsweetened cocoa powder

½ teaspoon baking soda

½ teaspoon salt

½ cup (1 stick) unsalted butter, softened

1 cup packed light brown sugar

1 large egg

1 tablespoon instant espresso powder mixed with 1 tablespoon water

8 ounces sour cream

1 cup white chocolate chips

DIRECTIONS

1. Preheat the oven to 350°F. Line two baking sheets with parchment paper.

2. In a medium bowl, combine the flour, cocoa powder, baking soda, and salt and set aside.

3. In a stand mixer fitted with the paddle attachment, cream the butter on medium-high speed for 2 minutes, then add the brown sugar and beat for an additional 3 minutes. Add the egg and espresso mixture and mix well. Alternate adding the dry ingredients and sour cream until well blended. Fold in the chips by hand.

4. Using a cookie scoop, shape the dough into 1-inch balls and place on the prepared baking sheets about 1½ inches apart. Bake for 12 to 15 minutes.

5. Cool on a wire rack. Store between layers of waxed paper or parchment paper in an airtight container.

Chocolate Chip Cookies 'n' Cream

Yield: 18–20 cookies | Prep Time: 20 minutes, plus 4 hours chilling time | Cook Time: 10–12 minutes

I love this cookie recipe because it's like having one of my all-time favorite ice cream flavors in a bite-size form. The smooth and creamy texture gets me every time!

INGREDIENTS

1 cup all-purpose flour

½ cup unsweetened cocoa powder

1 teaspoon baking soda

¼ teaspoon kosher salt

½ cup (1 stick) unsalted butter, softened

½ cup packed dark brown sugar

½ cup granulated sugar

1 large egg

1½ teaspoons vanilla extract

1 tablespoon whole milk

¼ cup white chocolate chips

¼ cup dark chocolate chips

DIRECTIONS

1. In a large bowl, combine the flour, cocoa powder, baking soda, and salt.

2. In a stand mixer fitted with the paddle attachment or in a large bowl using a hand mixer, beat the butter, brown sugar, and granulated sugar until creamy. Add the egg and vanilla and beat until well combined.

3. Add the flour mixture to the sugar mixture and beat until well combined.

4. Stir in the milk, then fold in the white chocolate chips and dark chocolate chips.

5. Cover and refrigerate for 4 hours or overnight.

6. Preheat the oven to 350°F. Line two baking sheets with parchment paper. Remove the dough from the refrigerator and let it sit while the oven is heating.

7. Using a cookie scoop, shape the dough into 2-inch balls and place them on the prepared baking sheets about 2 inches apart.

8. Bake for 10 to 12 minutes, until the edges are set.

9. Cool on the baking sheets for 10 minutes, then transfer to a wire rack to cool for 5 minutes more before serving.

Caramel Macchiato Cookies

Yield: 18 cookies | Prep Time: 10 minutes | Cook Time: 8–10 minutes

Those specialty drinks at the local coffee shop are dangerously delicious. It's so easy to find an excuse to pop in before work or during a lunch break. Sometimes when I'm feeling the urge for a sweet coffee treat, I bake a batch of these cookies to keep near my desk, so I can munch on them all day long.

INGREDIENTS

2 teaspoons instant espresso powder

1 tablespoon hot water

1 (17.5-ounce) bag sugar cookie mix

¼ cup all-purpose flour

½ cup unsalted butter, melted

2 teaspoons vanilla extract

¼ teaspoon salt

1 large egg

1 (12.25-ounce) jar caramel sauce

1 (11.75-ounce) jar hot fudge sauce

DIRECTIONS

1. Preheat the oven to 350°F. Coat two baking sheets with cooking spray. Set aside.

2. In a small bowl, dissolve the espresso powder into the hot water.

3. In a large bowl, combine the cookie mix and flour. Stir in the espresso mixture, butter, vanilla, salt, and egg until a soft dough forms.

4. Roll the dough into 1½-inch balls. Place on the baking sheets and bake for 8 to 10 minutes. Transfer to wire racks and cool completely. Lightly drizzle with caramel sauce and hot fudge. Place the cookies in the fridge for 5 to 10 minutes before serving to set the drizzle. Serve.

6

Old-Fashioned

It seems like you can find any outrageous flavor combination on the Internet these days just by mashing together all your favorite desserts into one ultimate mega-dessert. They can be super fun, but sometimes, you just need to take a breather and get back to basics. That's what these recipes are all about. They are the recipes you'd find in your grandmother's cookbook and munch on while enjoying a family night of Scrabble. Sometimes you don't need something over-the-top—you just need a classic that works every time.

Peanut Butter Pretzel Bites

Yield: 24 cookies | Prep Time: 20 minutes plus 30 minutes freezing time | Cook Time: 1 minute

These no-bake cookies are a divine treat to make when you're having a lazy night in and need a quick snack that you can munch on all night long. Throw the dough into the freezer to firm and pop in a movie—when you're ready to chow down, they're right there waiting for you!

INGREDIENTS

Cookies

1 cup creamy peanut butter

1 cup confectioners' sugar

1 tablespoon unsalted butter, softened

1 cup crushed pretzels

Toppings

1 cup dark chocolate chips

⅛ teaspoon instant espresso powder

DIRECTIONS

1. *For the cookies:* Line a baking sheet with waxed paper or parchment paper.

2. In a large bowl, combine the peanut butter, confectioners' sugar, butter, and crushed pretzels.

3. Using a cookie scoop, shape the dough into 1-inch balls and place on the prepared baking sheet about 1 inch apart. Freeze for 30 minutes or until firm.

4. *For the toppings:* In a small microwave-safe bowl, combine the dark chocolate chips and espresso powder. Microwave at 30-second intervals until fully melted.

5. Drizzle the melted chocolate over the pretzel bites. Serve.

VARIATIONS

Use crunchy peanut butter instead of creamy. Change up the type of chocolate chips: milk, semisweet, or white.

Russian Tea Cakes

Yield: 30 cookies | Prep Time: 10 minutes plus 1 hour chilling time | Cook Time: 25 minutes

Whether you know them as Mexican Wedding Cookies, Russian Tea Cakes, or Italian Almond Balls, these are a favorite treat around the world for holidays and special occasions. The confectioners'-sugar balls are light as a feather and will float right off the baking sheet into your mouth.

INGREDIENTS

1 cup chopped pecans

½ cup granulated sugar

½ teaspoon salt

1 cup (2 sticks) unsalted butter, cut into cubes and softened

1½ teaspoons vanilla extract

2 cups all-purpose flour

Confectioners' sugar

Ground cinnamon

DIRECTIONS

1. Preheat the oven to 325°F. Line a large baking sheet with parchment paper.

2. In a food processor, combine the pecans, granulated sugar, and salt. Pulse until the pecans are very finely ground. With the machine running, add the butter and process until the butter is well combined. Add the vanilla, then add the flour and pulse until well blended.

3. Transfer the dough to a bowl and chill, covered, for 1 hour or up to 1 day.

4. Using a cookie scoop, shape the dough into 1-inch balls. Dust your palms very lightly with flour and roll each into a smooth ball and place on the prepared baking sheet about 1½ inches apart.

5. Bake for 25 minutes, until the cookies just begin to brown.

6. Cool on the baking sheet on a wire rack until firm but still warm.

7. Sprinkle with the confectioners' sugar and cinnamon. Cool completely.

8. The cookies can be stored in an airtight container for 4 days or frozen for up to 1 month. If frozen, they may need to be coated with more of the confectioners' sugar–cinnamon mixture before serving.

Homemade Oatmeal Chocolate Chip Cookies

Yield: 48–60 cookies | Prep Time: 20 minutes | Cook Time: 9–10 minutes

I like finding little ways to work chocolate into my day: a splash of mocha coffee here and a bit of chocolate ice cream there. These made-from-scratch cookies satisfy my chocolate hankering.

INGREDIENTS

1 cup (2 sticks) unsalted butter, softened

1¼ cups packed light brown sugar

½ cup granulated sugar

2 large eggs

2 tablespoons whole milk

2 teaspoons vanilla extract

1¾ cups all-purpose flour

1 teaspoon baking soda

¼ teaspoon sea salt

1 teaspoon ground cinnamon

2½ cups rolled oats

1 cup semisweet chocolate chips

½ cup chopped pecans

DIRECTIONS

1. Preheat the oven to 375°F. Line two baking sheets with parchment paper.

2. In a large bowl, mix the butter, brown sugar, and granulated sugar until creamy. Add the eggs, milk, and vanilla.

3. In a separate large bowl, sift together the flour, baking soda, sea salt, and cinnamon. Add the flour mixture to the butter mixture and stir until well combined.

4. Stir in the oats, chocolate chips, and pecans.

5. Using a cookie scoop, shape the dough into 1-inch balls and place on the prepared baking sheets about 2 inches apart.

6. Bake for 9 to 10 minutes for a chewy cookie or 11 to 13 minutes for a crispier cookie.

7. Cool for 10 minutes before serving.

Half-Moon Cookies

Yield: 24 cookies | Prep Time: 30 minutes | Cook Time: 20 minutes

Any time I visit New York, I can't resist stopping in a bakery to pick up a few Half-Moon Cookies. I love knowing that I have this recipe to turn to and bring the taste of New York home.

INGREDIENTS

Cookies

2 cups cake flour

2 cups all-purpose flour

½ teaspoon baking powder

½ teaspoon salt

½ cup (1 stick) unsalted butter, softened

½ cup vegetable shortening, softened

1¾ cups granulated sugar

2 large eggs

1 cup whole milk

½ teaspoon vanilla extract

Glaze

6 tablespoons water

¼ cup light corn syrup

5 cups confectioners' sugar

½ teaspoon vanilla extract

2 ounces dark chocolate chips or melts

DIRECTIONS

1. *For the cookies:* Preheat the oven to 375°F. Line two baking sheets with parchment paper.

2. In a medium bowl, using a whisk, stir together the cake flour, all-purpose flour, baking powder, and salt.

3. In a stand mixer fitted with the paddle attachment, beat the butter, shortening, and granulated sugar on medium-high speed for about 3 minutes, scraping down the sides of the bowl once.

4. With the mixer running, add the eggs, milk, and vanilla in alternating batches with the flour mixture, ending with the flour mixture. Scrape down the sides of the bowl—the dough will have the consistency of cake batter.

5. Using a cookie scoop, shape the dough into 2-inch rounds and place them on the prepared baking sheets 2 to 3 inches apart. Bake for about 20 minutes until the edges just begin to brown.

6. Cool on the baking sheets for 2 minutes, then transfer to wire racks to cool completely before glazing.

7. *For the glaze:* In a small saucepan, combine the water and corn syrup and bring to a boil over medium heat. Immediately stir in the confectioners' sugar and vanilla and whisk to make a smooth, translucent glaze.

8. Use an offset spatula to ice one half of each cookie with the glaze.

9. Meanwhile, put the chocolate chips in a small bowl and microwave on 40% power in 30-second increments, stirring after each. Stir the chocolate into the remaining glaze and ice the second half of each cookie. Transfer the cookies to wire racks to set completely. Serve.

Old-Fashioned Pecan Pie Cheesecake Bars

Yield: 24 cookies | Prep Time: 30 minutes plus 4 hours chilling time | Cook Time: 45 minutes

Nothing says "fall" quite like a classic pecan pie. This cheesecake bar version takes the holiday favorite you know and love and transforms it into a to-go version, perfect for bake sales . . . or even just to enjoy yourself!

INGREDIENTS

Shortbread Crust

1½ cups all-purpose flour

¾ cup packed light brown sugar

½ cup (1 stick) unsalted butter, softened

½ cup chopped pecans

Cheesecake Layer

16 ounces cream cheese, softened

¾ cup granulated sugar

2 large eggs

1 teaspoon vanilla extract

Pecan Pie Layer

1 cup packed light brown sugar

½ cup light corn syrup

½ cup heavy cream

4 tablespoons (½ stick) unsalted butter

½ teaspoon kosher salt

1 teaspoon vanilla extract

2 cups pecans, chopped

DIRECTIONS

1. *For the shortbread crust:* Preheat the oven to 350°F. Line a 9 × 13-inch baking dish with parchment paper.

2. In a large bowl, combine the flour and brown sugar. Cut in the butter until the mixture resembles coarse crumbs. Mix in the pecans. Press into the baking dish in an even layer and bake for 10 minutes. Cool for 10 minutes.

3. *For the cheesecake layer:* In a separate large bowl, combine the cream cheese, granulated sugar, eggs, and vanilla. Beat until smooth, 3 to 5 minutes. Pour over the cooled crust.

4. *For the pecan pie layer:* In a small saucepan, combine the brown sugar, corn syrup, cream, butter, and salt and bring to a boil over medium heat. Once it's boiling, stir for 1 minute. Remove from the heat and add the vanilla and pecans. Pour over the cheesecake layer.

5. Bake for 35 minutes. Let the cheesecake fully cool, then refrigerate for 4 hours or up to 4 days.

6. Cut into bars and serve.

Nana's Best Coconut Macaroons

Yield: 24 cookies | Prep Time: 20 minutes | Cook Time: 22–25 minutes

My nana always seemed to have some sort of baked good ready to go. It was astounding—her cookie jar was never empty! Maybe it was because they looked so fancy, but her coconut macaroons were always a special treat.

INGREDIENTS

1 (14-ounce) bag sweetened shredded coconut

¾ cup plus 2 tablespoons sweetened condensed milk

1 teaspoon vanilla extract

2 large egg whites, at room temperature

¼ teaspoon salt

DIRECTIONS

1. Preheat the oven to 325°F. Line two baking sheets with parchment paper.

2. In a large bowl, combine the shredded coconut, condensed milk, and vanilla and mix well.

3. In a small bowl using a hand mixer, beat the egg whites with the salt until they hold stiff peaks.

4. Carefully fold the egg whites and salt into the coconut mixture.

5. Using a cookie scoop, shape the dough into 1-inch balls and place on the prepared baking sheets about 1 inch apart.

6. Bake for 22 to 25 minutes, until the tops are lightly browned and the bottoms are golden brown. Cool and serve.

Chewy Classic Oatmeal Raisin Cookies

Yield: 24 cookies | Prep Time: 45 minutes, including chilling time | Cook Time: 10 minutes

It's perfectly acceptable to enjoy cookies for breakfast, wouldn't you agree? When you add in oats, they become fair game. Grab a few when you're rushing out the door, and you've got yourself breakfast on-the-go!

INGREDIENTS

1 cup (2 sticks) unsalted butter, softened

1 cup packed light brown sugar

¼ cup granulated sugar

2 large eggs

1 tablespoon vanilla extract

1 tablespoon molasses

1½ cups all-purpose flour

1 teaspoon baking soda

1½ teaspoons ground cinnamon

½ teaspoon salt

3 cups old-fashioned rolled oats

½ cup golden raisins

½ cup dried cranberries

½ cup chopped pecans

DIRECTIONS

1. Preheat the oven to 350°F. Line two baking sheets with parchment paper.

2. In a stand mixer fitted with the paddle attachment or in a large bowl using a hand mixer, cream the butter, brown sugar, and granulated sugar on medium-high speed for 2 minutes. Add the eggs and beat to combine. Add the vanilla and molasses and mix well.

3. In a large bowl, combine the flour, baking soda, cinnamon, and salt. Slowly add the flour mixture to the sugar mixture and mix until combined.

4. Add the oats, raisins, cranberries, and pecans.

5. Chill the dough for 30 minutes or longer if needed.

6. Using a cookie scoop, shape the dough into 1-inch balls and place on the prepared baking sheets about 2 inches apart.

7. Bake for 10 minutes, until lightly golden.

8. Cool for 5 minutes, then transfer to a wire rack to cool completely. Serve.

Turtle Thumbprint Cookies

Yield: 24 cookies | Prep Time: 15 minutes plus 1 hour chilling time | Cook Time: 12 minutes

Turtle desserts are the ultimate indulgence, and these turtle cookies are worth it. When you combine classic turtles with thumbprint cookies, you get a modern marvel.

INGREDIENTS

1 large egg

2 tablespoons milk

1 teaspoon vanilla extract

1 cup all-purpose flour

⅓ cup unsweetened cocoa powder

¼ teaspoon salt

½ cup (1 stick) unsalted butter, softened

⅔ cup sugar

1 cup pecans, finely chopped

6 caramel candies

Flaked sea salt (optional)

¼ cup semisweet chocolate chips

½ teaspoon vegetable oil

DIRECTIONS

1. Separate the egg, setting aside the white in a small, covered bowl. In a small bowl, combine the yolk, milk, and vanilla.

2. In another small bowl, sift together the flour, cocoa powder, and salt.

3. In a stand mixer fitted with the paddle attachment, beat the butter on medium-high speed for 2 minutes until smooth, then add the sugar and beat for an additional 2 minutes, until light and fluffy. Add the egg yolk mixture and beat until blended. With the mixer running on medium speed, gradually add the flour mixture until well blended. Turn the dough out onto a piece of plastic wrap and roll it into a log about 1½ inches in diameter. Wrap the log in the plastic wrap and chill for 1 hour or up to 12 hours.

4. When ready to bake, preheat the oven to 350°F. Line two baking sheets with parchment paper.

5. Put the pecans in a small bowl. Use a fork to lightly beat the reserved egg white. Slice the log crosswise into 24 pieces. Roll each piece in the egg white and then in the chopped pecans. Place on the prepared baking sheets 1 inch apart and use your thumb or the back of a measuring spoon to make an indention in each. Cut each caramel candy into quarters and press one quarter into each cookie. Sprinkle each cookie with a bit of sea salt, if desired. Bake for about 12 minutes. Cool on a wire rack.

6. When the cookies are cool, combine the chocolate chips and vegetable oil in a small microwave-safe bowl and microwave in 30-second intervals, stirring after each, until melted. Stir until smooth, then use the tip of a spoon to drizzle lines of chocolate across each cookie. Serve.

Chewy Molasses Cookies

Yield: 30 cookies | Prep Time: 15 minutes plus 30 minutes chilling time | Cook Time: 8–10 minutes

These soft, chewy cookies store well, which makes them a prime cookie jar treat. The combination of sweet molasses and dry mustard makes for the perfect flavor pairing—trust me! Plus, if you want to really fancy them up, spread ice cream between two of the cookies to create your very own ice cream sandwich.

INGREDIENTS

4 cups all-purpose flour

4 teaspoons baking soda

2 teaspoons ground cinnamon

1 teaspoon salt

1 teaspoon ground ginger

¼ teaspoon ground cloves

¼ teaspoon dry mustard

1½ cups (3 sticks) unsalted butter, softened

2¼ cups sugar

½ cup molasses

2 large eggs

DIRECTIONS

1. In a medium bowl, combine the flour, baking soda, cinnamon, salt, ginger, cloves, and mustard. Toss with a fork to mix well.

2. In a stand mixer fitted with the paddle attachment, beat the butter on medium-high speed for 2 minutes. Add 2 cups of the sugar and beat for 3 minutes, scraping down the bowl once. Add the molasses and eggs and beat briefly, then with the machine running on low, gradually add the flour mixture and beat until well combined. Cover the bowl with plastic wrap and chill in the refrigerator for 30 minutes or up to 12 hours.

3. Preheat the oven to 375°F. Line two baking sheets with parchment paper.

4. Put the remaining ¼ cup sugar in a small bowl. Using a cookie scoop, shape the dough into 2-inch balls. Drop them into the sugar and roll to coat. Place on the prepared baking sheets about 2 inches apart. Press lightly with the bottom of a glass or cup. Bake for 8 to 10 minutes.

5. Cool on the baking sheet for 3 to 5 minutes, then transfer to a wire rack to cool completely.

6. Store in an airtight container at room temperature for up to 1 week.

Classic French Madeleines

Yield: 20–22 cookies | Prep Time: 10 minutes | Cook Time: 12–14 minutes

This French cookie delicacy pairs wonderfully with your afternoon tea out on the front porch. I love making these for my niece's tea parties to add an authentic touch.

INGREDIENTS

2 large eggs

⅔ cup granulated sugar

1 teaspoon vanilla or almond extract

½ teaspoon lemon zest

Pinch of sea salt

1 cup all-purpose flour

10 tablespoons (1¼ sticks) unsalted butter, melted and cooled

Confectioners' sugar for dusting

DIRECTIONS

1. Preheat the oven to 375°F. Butter and flour a nonstick madeleine pan.

2. In a stand mixer fitted with the paddle attachment or in a medium bowl using a hand mixer, beat the eggs and granulated sugar until blended. Beat in the vanilla, lemon zest, and sea salt.

3. Add the flour and beat until blended. Gradually add the butter slowly until blended.

4. Spoon 1 tablespoon of the batter into each indentation in the prepared pan.

5. Bake until puffy and brown, 12 to 14 minutes.

6. Cool for 5 minutes. Carefully remove from the pan.

7. Let the pan cool. Repeat the process with the remainder of the batter.

8. Dust with confectioners' sugar. Serve.

3-Ingredient Old-Fashioned Shortbread Buttons

Yield: 20 cookies | Prep Time: 5 minutes | Cook Time: 15 minutes

Sometimes the best cookies are the simplest ones. Old-fashioned shortbread cookies only need three ingredients to be buttery and delicious. If you want to spruce them up, the small indent in the center lets you add your favorite filling, like chocolate-hazelnut spread or frosting.

INGREDIENTS

1 cup (2 sticks) unsalted butter, softened

½ cup confectioners' sugar

2 cups all-purpose flour

DIRECTIONS

1. Preheat the oven to 350°F. Line a baking sheet with parchment paper.

2. In a large bowl, cream together the butter and confectioners' sugar.

3. Add the flour and mix until a soft dough forms.

4. Using a cookie scoop, shape the dough into 1-inch balls and place on the prepared baking sheet about 2 inches apart.

5. Using your thumb, make a small indentation in the center of each cookie.

6. Bake for 15 minutes, or until lightly golden. Feel free to fill the indentation with chocolate-hazelnut spread or frosting. Serve.

Breakfast Cookies

Yield: 24 cookies | Prep Time: 25 minutes | Cook Time: 8–10 minutes

If you say I can have an old-fashioned oatmeal cookie for breakfast and it has all the protein and fiber I need to jump-start my day, then I say hooray! Filled with whole wheat flour and flax meal, this is a good-for-you treat that will quickly become a fixture of your morning routine.

INGREDIENTS

1 cup walnuts

1½ cups old-fashioned rolled oats (not instant)

⅓ cup whole wheat flour

½ cup flax meal

1 teaspoon baking soda

½ teaspoon salt

1 teaspoon ground cinnamon, plus extra for topping

½ cup creamy peanut butter

¼ cup canola oil

¼ cup blue agave nectar

⅓ cup packed light brown sugar

1 large egg

1 teaspoon vanilla extract

½ cup dried cherries

1 cup semisweet chocolate chips

DIRECTIONS

1. Preheat the oven to 375°F. Line two baking sheets with parchment paper.

2. Pulse the walnuts in a food processor several times to chop; continue processing until the walnuts are ground into flour; transfer to a bowl. Mix in the oats, whole wheat flour, flax meal, baking soda, salt, and cinnamon until thoroughly combined.

3. Combine the peanut butter, canola oil, agave nectar, brown sugar, egg, and vanilla in the food processor and process for a few seconds to blend the ingredients well; transfer the peanut butter mixture to a large bowl and fold in the dried cherries and chocolate chips. Mix the walnut-oatmeal mixture into the peanut butter mixture.

4. Using a cookie scoop, shape the dough into 1½-inch balls and place on the prepared baking sheets about 2 inches apart.

5. Bake until lightly browned, 8 to 10 minutes.

6. Remove from the oven and flatten the cookies with a spatula. Cool for about 5 minutes on the baking sheets and sprinkle with cinnamon before serving.

Red Velvet Thumbprints

Yield: 36 cookies | Prep Time: 20 minutes | Cook Time: 12 minutes

Red is the color of love, and these rich red velvet cookies have affection written all over them. Red velvet cake was a popular dessert trend in the '40s and '50s, and it's fun to create a cookie version! Make a batch of these timeless classics for Valentine's Day or Christmas, and show your friends and family just how much you care.

INGREDIENTS

Cookies

1 cup (2 sticks) unsalted butter, softened

2 cups granulated sugar

2 large eggs

2 teaspoons vanilla extract

3¾ cups all-purpose flour

¼ cup unsweetened cocoa powder

½ teaspoon kosher salt

½ teaspoon baking soda

½ teaspoon baking powder

1½–2 tablespoons red food coloring

Cream Cheese Filling

2 tablespoons unsalted butter, softened

4 ounces cream cheese, softened

½ teaspoon vanilla extract

2 cups confectioners' sugar

DIRECTIONS

1. *For the cookies:* Preheat the oven to 350°F. Line two baking sheets with parchment paper.

2. In a large bowl, cream the butter and granulated sugar until smooth. Mix in the eggs. Add the vanilla and mix well.

3. Add the flour, cocoa powder, salt, baking soda, and baking powder and mix until combined. Add the red food coloring and mix well.

4. Using a cookie scoop, shape the dough into 1-inch balls and place on the prepared baking sheets about 2 inches apart.

5. Gently press the center of each cookie with your thumb or the back of a measuring spoon to create a depression.

6. Bake the cookies for 12 minutes.

7. Cool the cookies on the baking sheets for 2 minutes, then transfer to a wire rack to cool completely.

8. *For the cream cheese filling:* In a small bowl, mix the butter and cream cheese until light and fluffy. Mix in the vanilla. Gradually add the confectioners' sugar and mix until smooth.

9. Pipe or scoop the cream cheese filling into the indentation in each cookie. Serve.

Toffee Butter Icebox Cookies

Yield: 48 cookies | Prep Time: 15 minutes plus 1–2 hours chilling time | Cook Time: 8 minutes

Icebox cookies are just what you need to have around when you're in a baking bind. If you're expecting guests and have plenty of other courses to cook, then you can save a bit of time by prepping the cookie dough ahead of time, so you only need to slice and bake! I like to keep a few rolls of these on hand in my freezer for impromptu get-togethers, just like my grandma used to do.

INGREDIENTS

1 cup (2 sticks) unsalted butter, softened

½ cup granulated sugar

½ cup packed light brown sugar

1 large egg

1 teaspoon vanilla extract

2½ cups all-purpose flour

⅛ teaspoon kosher salt

¾ cup Heath toffee chips

½ cup chopped pecans

DIRECTIONS

1. In a large bowl, cream the butter, granulated sugar, and brown sugar with a hand mixer on medium-high speed until combined.

2. Add the egg and vanilla and mix well.

3. Slowly add the flour and kosher salt and mix until combined.

4. Fold in the Heath toffee chips and pecans.

5. Divide the dough in half. Form each piece into a log about 6 inches long and 1½ inches around.

6. Wrap the dough logs in plastic wrap and chill for 1 to 2 hours.

7. Preheat the oven to 375°F. Line two baking sheets with parchment paper.

8. Cut the logs crosswise into ¼-inch-thick slices and place on the prepared baking sheets 2 inches apart.

9. Bake for 8 minutes, or until browned.

10. Cool on the baking sheets for a few minutes, then transfer to a wire rack to cool completely. Serve.

Ricotta Cookies

Yield: 30 cookies | Prep Time: 20 minutes | Cook Time: 12–15 minutes

Sure, it's not unusual to see a dessert recipe using cream cheese, but have you ever tried one with ricotta? Trust me—this recipe is incredible. If you're already picking up some ricotta cheese for lasagna night, get some extra and try out this dish for dessert.

INGREDIENTS

Cookies

1 cup (2 sticks) unsalted butter, softened

2 cups granulated sugar

2 large eggs

15 ounces ricotta cheese

1 teaspoons lemon zest

2 teaspoons lemon juice

4 cups all-purpose flour

2 teaspoons baking powder

1 teaspoon salt

Glaze

1 cup confectioners' sugar

Pinch of salt

1–2 teaspoons lemon zest

2 teaspoons lemon juice

Whipped topping for garnish

Silver sugar pearls for garnish

DIRECTIONS

1. *For the cookies:* Preheat the oven to 350°F. Line two baking sheets with parchment paper.

2. In a stand mixer fitted with the paddle attachment, combine the butter and granulated sugar and beat on medium-high speed for 3 minutes, until very fluffy and light. Add the eggs one at a time with the machine running, stopping to scrape down the sides after each addition. Add the ricotta cheese, lemon zest, and lemon juice and mix.

3. In a medium bowl, combine the flour, baking powder, and salt and toss to mix. With the stand mixer running on medium-low, gradually add the flour mixture to the ricotta cheese mixture until well combined.

4. Using a cookie scoop, shape the dough into 1-inch balls and place on the prepared baking sheets about 1 inch apart. Smooth the tops with a dampened finger and bake for 12 to 15 minutes. The cookies will remain very pale colored, but they will be firm on the top and very lightly golden on the bottom.

5. Cool on the baking sheets set on a wire rack for 2 minutes, then transfer the cookies directly to the wire rack to cool completely.

6. *For the glaze:* In a small bowl, combine the confectioners' sugar, salt, lemon zest, and lemon juice, adding water if necessary to make a pourable glaze. Dip the cookies into the glaze and place back on the wire rack until the glaze is set. Serve with whipped topping and silver sugar pearls.

Soft Peanut Butter Cookies

Yield: 12–16 cookies | Prep Time: 5 minutes | Cook Time: 10–11 minutes

There is something so special about the simplicity of the peanut butter cookie. They remind me of childhood, go great with a glass of milk after a tough day, and are so easy to make. The combination of peanut butter, sugar, and vanilla practically melts in your mouth. Make a double batch because these disappear fast!

INGREDIENTS

1 cup creamy peanut butter

1 cup sugar

1 large egg

1 teaspoon vanilla extract

Pinch of salt

DIRECTIONS

1. Preheat the oven to 325°F. Line two baking sheets with parchment paper.

2. In a medium bowl using a hand mixer, combine all of the ingredients and mix until blended. Do not overmix or the cookies will be tough. Using your hands, shape the dough into 1½-inch balls and place on the prepared baking sheets about 2 inches apart. Press a crisscross pattern onto each cookie with a fork.

3. Bake for 10 to 11 minutes, or until lightly golden just around the edges.

4. Cool completely on the baking sheets and serve.

7

Holiday

Everyone needs a few holiday cookie recipes to keep in
their back pocket for the various office cookie exchanges, Yankee
swaps, and family gatherings that book up your calendar in December.
These homemade treats are made with love and allow you to truly
get into the spirit of sharing and giving during the holiday season.

3-Ingredient Pumpkin Cake Cookies

Yield: 24 cookies | Prep Time: 5 minutes | Cook Time: 10–15 minutes

There's no better season for baking than fall. Between apples and pumpkins, you've pretty much got dessert all figured out for three months straight. I always turn to this recipe when I see the leaves start to change color, and I'm ready to dive headfirst into a fall frenzy.

INGREDIENTS

1 (15.25-ounce) box spice cake mix

1 (15-ounce) can pure pumpkin puree

¼ cup maple syrup

DIRECTIONS

1. Preheat the oven to 375°F. Line a baking sheet with parchment paper.

2. In a large bowl, mix together the cake mix and pumpkin puree until well combined.

3. Using a cookie scoop, shape the dough into 1-inch balls and place on the prepared baking sheet about 2 inches apart.

4. Bake for 10 to 15 minutes until set. Cool.

5. Drizzle the maple syrup over the cookies. Serve.

Christmas Magic Squares

Yield: 20 squares | Prep Time: 15–20 minutes | Cook Time: 30 minutes

It's hard to know what the most magical part of this recipe is: the fact that it doesn't require any mixing bowls, the sweetness of the coconut and condensed milk, or the satisfying crunch in every bite! These layered cookie bars will be gone before Santa even has a chance to try one.

INGREDIENTS

½ cup (1 stick) unsalted butter

1½ cups graham cracker crumbs

1 (10-ounce) package holiday dark chocolate and mint chips

1 cup chopped walnuts

½ cup toffee bits

1 cup sweetened shredded coconut

1 (14-ounce) can sweetened condensed milk

½ cup red and green chocolate-covered candies

DIRECTIONS

1. Preheat the oven to 350°F.

2. Place the butter in a 9 × 13-inch baking dish. Place the dish in the oven for 3 to 5 minutes to melt the butter.

3. Layer the graham cracker crumbs, holiday dark chocolate and mint chips, walnuts, toffee bits, and shredded coconut over the butter.

4. Pour the condensed milk over the coconut. Top with the red and green chocolate-covered candies.

5. Bake for 30 minutes. Cool, then cut into squares to serve.

Peppermint Crunch Balls

Yield: 36 cookies | Prep Time: 30 minutes plus 1 hour chilling time | Cook Time: 10–12 minutes

Turn on your favorite Christmas movie, light up the Christmas tree, and munch on these peppermint cookies to truly enjoy the spirit of the holiday season. Pair these with a mug of hot cocoa for a late-night Christmas twinkle.

INGREDIENTS

1 cup (2 sticks) unsalted butter, softened

1 cup confectioners' sugar

1 large egg

½ teaspoon peppermint extract

½ teaspoon vanilla extract

2½ cups all-purpose flour

¼ teaspoon salt

6 Andes mints, chopped

1 cup finely crushed round peppermint candies (or candy canes)

3 tablespoons granulated sugar

DIRECTIONS

1. In a large bowl, cream the butter and confectioners' sugar using a hand mixer on medium-high speed until light and fluffy.

2. Add the egg, peppermint extract, and vanilla and mix until blended.

3. Slowly add the flour and salt and mix until well combined. Fold in the Andes mints.

4. Cover the bowl and refrigerate for 1 hour.

5. Preheat the oven to 350°F. Line two baking sheets with parchment paper.

6. Combine the crushed candy canes with the sugar in a small bowl. Using a cookie scoop, shape the dough into 1-inch balls. Roll each cookie ball in the candy cane mixture and place on the prepared baking sheets about 2 inches apart.

7. Bake for 10 to 12 minutes, until golden.

8. Cool on wire racks. Serve.

North Pole Lemon Cookies

Yield: 36 cookies | Prep Time: 20 minutes | Cook Time: 12–15 minutes

Topped with white Christmas vanilla frosting, these sweet lemon cookies are good enough for Mrs. Claus's kitchen! It's easy to get bogged down with chocolate, caramel, and the whole she-bang during the holidays, which is why a fruity cookie like this can be such a refreshing choice.

INGREDIENTS

2½ cups all-purpose flour

¾ cup granulated sugar

2½ teaspoons baking powder

½ cup vegetable oil

½ cup whole milk

Pinch of salt

1 tablespoon lemon extract

1 teaspoon lemon zest

1 large egg

1 (16-ounce) tub of vanilla frosting

DIRECTIONS

1. Preheat the oven to 350°F. Line two baking sheets with parchment paper.

2. In a large bowl, combine the flour, granulated sugar, baking powder, vegetable oil, milk, salt, lemon extract, lemon zest, and egg.

3. Using a cookie scoop, shape the dough into 1½-inch balls and place on the prepared baking sheets about 2 inches apart.

4. Bake for 12 to 15 minutes until the cookies are set but not brown.

5. Let set for 5 minutes. Transfer to a wire rack to cool.

6. Top with vanilla frosting and serve.

Jolly Holly Cookies

Yield: 36 cookies | Prep Time: 15 minutes plus 30 minutes setting time | Cook Time: 5–10 minutes

These green cookies are sure to pop when you lay them out on the Christmas dessert table! Pair these with Red Velvet Thumbprints (page 185) to create a red-and-green platter that's befitting of Christmas.

INGREDIENTS

½ cup (1 stick) unsalted butter

30 large marshmallows

1 teaspoon green food coloring, more if darker color desired

1½ teaspoons vanilla extract

4 cups cornflakes

Red-hot cinnamon candies

DIRECTIONS

1. Line two baking sheets with parchment paper.

2. In a large saucepan, combine the butter and marshmallows and heat over medium-low heat, stirring continuously until everything has melted.

3. Remove from the heat and stir in the green food coloring and vanilla.

4. Stir in the cornflakes.

5. Using a cookie scoop, shape the dough into 1-inch balls and place on the prepared baking sheets about 1 inch apart. Decorate with red-hot cinnamon candies.

6. Let stand for 30 minutes until set. Serve.

Easy Pecan Pie Bars

Yield: 24 bars | Prep Time: 15–20 minutes | Cook Time: 20–25 minutes

Have you ever tried baking desserts with crescent roll dough before? It's such a time-saver in the kitchen! Skip the arduous task of making a whole pie by making these handy shortcut cookie bars instead.

INGREDIENTS

1 (8-ounce) package refrigerated crescent rolls

¼ cup granulated sugar

¼ cup packed light brown sugar

¾ cup chopped pecans

¾ cup corn syrup

1 large egg, beaten

1 tablespoon unsalted butter, melted

½ teaspoon vanilla extract

Pinch of sea salt

DIRECTIONS

1. Preheat the oven to 375°F. Coat a 9 × 13-inch baking dish with cooking spray.

2. Separate the dough into two large dough rectangles and press over the bottom and up the sides of the prepared baking dish. Press to seal the perforations. Bake for 5 minutes.

3. Combine the remaining ingredients in a bowl and mix well. Pour over the crust.

4. Bake for 15 to 20 minutes, until the crust is golden and the filling is set.

5. Cool, then cut into bars to serve.

Italian Christmas Cookies

Yield: 24 cookies | Prep Time: 10 minutes | Cook Time: 12–15 minutes

One of my best friends growing up was Italian, and I loved helping her and her mom make a fresh batch of Italian Christmas cookies during the holidays. We would eat so many that there'd hardly be any left for the rest of her family! It's a holiday tradition I cherish to this day.

INGREDIENTS

Cookies

1 (8-ounce) can crushed pineapple in juice

2 cups all-purpose flour

1½ teaspoons baking powder

½ teaspoon ground nutmeg

¼ teaspoon baking soda

½ cup (1 stick) unsalted butter

1 cup packed light brown sugar

1 large egg

1 teaspoon vanilla extract

Frosting/Glaze

1½ teaspoons confectioners' sugar

½ teaspoon salt

¼ teaspoon vanilla extract

Sprinkles or Demerara sugar (optional)

DIRECTIONS

1. *For the cookies:* Preheat the oven to 350°F. Line two baking sheets with parchment paper.

2. Drain the crushed pineapple, reserving 1 tablespoon of the juice for the glaze. In a medium bowl, sift together the flour, baking powder, ground nutmeg, and baking soda.

3. In a stand mixer fitted with the paddle attachment, beat the butter on medium-high speed for 2 minutes until light and fluffy. Add the brown sugar and beat for 2 minutes more. Add the egg and vanilla and mix until well blended. With the mixer running on medium, gradually add the dry ingredients until well mixed.

4. Using a cookie scoop, shape the dough into 2-inch balls and place on the prepared baking sheets 2 inches apart. Bake for 12 to 15 minutes until lightly browned.

5. Cool completely on wire racks.

6. *For the frosting/glaze:* While the cookies cool, combine the confectioners' sugar and salt in a medium bowl. Stir in the vanilla and the reserved pineapple juice to make a light glaze.

7. Use an offset spatula to smooth some glaze on each cookie. Top with sprinkles or Demerara sugar (optional). Serve.

Stained Glass Window Cookies

Yield: 24 cookies | Prep Time: 5 minutes plus 2 hours chilling time | Cook Time: 5 minutes

If you're looking for the best no-bake cookie recipe to bring to your Christmas church services or your Christmas Eve festivities, these classy treats are just what you need! The shredded coconut reminds me of a peaceful winter night when, for a moment, everything feels just right.

INGREDIENTS

½ cup (1 stick) unsalted butter

1 (12-ounce) package semisweet chocolate chips

1 teaspoon vanilla extract

½ teaspoon salt

1 cup chopped walnuts

1 (10.5-ounce) package mini marshmallows

1 cup sweetened shredded coconut

DIRECTIONS

1. In a large saucepan, melt the butter and semisweet chocolate chips over low heat. Remove the saucepan from the heat and add the vanilla, salt, and walnuts. Cool for 15 minutes.

2. Add the marshmallows and stir until combined.

3. Spoon half the mixture lengthwise down the center of a piece of waxed paper and roll it into a log. Sprinkle the coconut on and roll the log, evenly coating the outside. Wrap the log in waxed paper. Repeat with the remaining dough.

4. Chill for at least 2 hours.

5. Unwrap and slice into ¼-inch slices and serve.

Chocolate Kiss Surprise Powder Puff Cookies

Yield: 15 cookies | Prep Time: 10 minutes | Cook Time: 15–17 minutes

There's not always time to prepare a fancy dish for dessert. When you've got a roast in the slow cooker and mashed potatoes on the stovetop and the phone's ringing in the other room, three-ingredient desserts like these can feel like a real lifesaver.

INGREDIENTS

1 frozen pie dough round, for a 9-inch pie, thawed

15 chocolate-almond kisses

Sugar for rolling

DIRECTIONS

1. Preheat the oven to 350°F. Line a baking sheet with parchment paper or coat with cooking spray.

2. Place the pie dough on a lightly floured surface and, using a pizza wheel, slice it into about 16 roughly 2-inch squares.

3. Place one chocolate-almond kiss in the center of each square. Using your fingertips, seal the dough at the top to fully contain the kiss. Place the mound on the prepared baking sheet; repeat with the remaining dough and kisses.

4. Lightly roll in sugar.

5. Bake for 15 to 17 minutes, or until the crust is just set and done; the puffs firm up as they cool.

6. Cool on the baking sheet for about 15 minutes.

7. Serve. The puffs will keep in an airtight container at room temperature for up to 1 week or in the freezer for up to 4 months.

Pizzelles

Yield: 36 cookies | Prep Time: 10 minutes | Cook Time: 9 minutes

These crisp, buttery Italian cookies are ideal for a last-minute holiday gift. I love to make a whole bunch of them and wrap them up in bundles with colorful plastic baggies and fancy ribbons. Hand them out along with a recipe card, and you've got yourself the perfect little gift for the neighbors, mailman, coworkers, and more!

INGREDIENTS

6 large eggs

1 cup (2 sticks) unsalted butter, melted

1½ cups granulated sugar

½ teaspoon sea salt

2 teaspoons vanilla extract

3½ cups all-purpose flour

Confectioners' sugar (optional)

DIRECTIONS

1. In a large bowl, beat the eggs until they're pale and thick. Add the melted butter and mix until well combined. Mix in the granulated sugar until combined. Add the sea salt. Add the vanilla and mix. Slowly add the flour until just combined.

2. Preheat a pizzelle iron according to the manufacturer's directions.

3. Drop the batter by heaping tablespoonfuls onto the iron. Close the iron and cook for 30–40 seconds, in batches. Adjust the time for lighter or darker pizzelles.

4. With a rubber spatula, transfer the pizzelles to a wire rack. Repeat with the remainder of the batter.

5. Dust with confectioners' sugar, if desired. Serve.

Unforgettable White Chocolate Cranberry Cookies

Yield: 24–30 cookies | Prep Time: 15 minutes | Cook Time: 10–12 minutes

Cranberries mark the start of the holiday season. I like to wait until the grocery store has a big sale on cranberries, usually just after Thanksgiving, and then stock up to make all of my favorite festive dishes. Believe me—your friends and family will be munching on these throughout the entire month of December.

INGREDIENTS

¾ cup (1½ sticks) unsalted butter, melted

1 cup packed light brown sugar

½ cup granulated sugar

2 large eggs

1 teaspoon vanilla extract

2¼ cups all-purpose flour

½ teaspoon baking soda

½ teaspoon kosher salt

¾ cup white chocolate chips or chunks

1 cup dried cranberries

½ cup macadamia nuts, chopped

DIRECTIONS

1. Preheat the oven to 375°F. Line two baking sheets with parchment paper.

2. In a large bowl, beat the melted butter, brown sugar, and granulated sugar using a hand mixer on medium-high speed until smooth. Beat in the eggs one at a time. Add the vanilla. Slowly add the flour, baking soda, and salt. Fold in the chocolate chips, cranberries, and macadamia nuts.

3. Using a cookie scoop, shape the dough into 1-inch balls and place on the prepared baking sheets about 2 inches apart.

4. Bake for 10 to 12 minutes.

5. Cool on wire racks. Serve.

Gingerbread People

Yield: 12 cookies | Prep Time: 10 minutes plus 2 hours chilling time | Cook Time: 8–10 minutes

As a child, I remember watching my aunt make these and hang them on the banister in the weeks leading up to Christmas. My uncle used to walk up the stairs and occasionally eat a head off. I thought it was hilarious, but my aunt, on the other hand, did not. This is a soft, chewy version of her holiday classic.

INGREDIENTS

1 (15.25-ounce) box spice-flavored cake mix

½ cup all-purpose flour, plus more for rolling

2 teaspoons ground ginger

2 large eggs

⅓ cup vegetable oil

½ cup dark molasses

Assorted candies and icing for decorating

DIRECTIONS

1. In a stand mixer fitted with the paddle attachment, combine the spice-flavored cake mix, ½ cup flour, and ground ginger and mix on low for a few seconds to combine. In a small bowl, combine the eggs, vegetable oil, and dark molasses, beating briefly. Then add to the flour mixture with the machine on medium. Beat for 2 minutes, scraping down the sides once. Cover the bowl with plastic wrap and chill for 2 hours or up to 3 days before continuing.

2. Preheat the oven to 375°F. Line two baking sheets with parchment paper.

3. On a lightly floured work surface, roll the dough in two batches to ¼-inch thickness. Cut with cookie cutters and place on the baking sheet about 1½ inches apart. Bake for 8 to 10 minutes, until the edges just begin to brown.

4. Cool completely on a wire rack before decorating as desired. Serve.

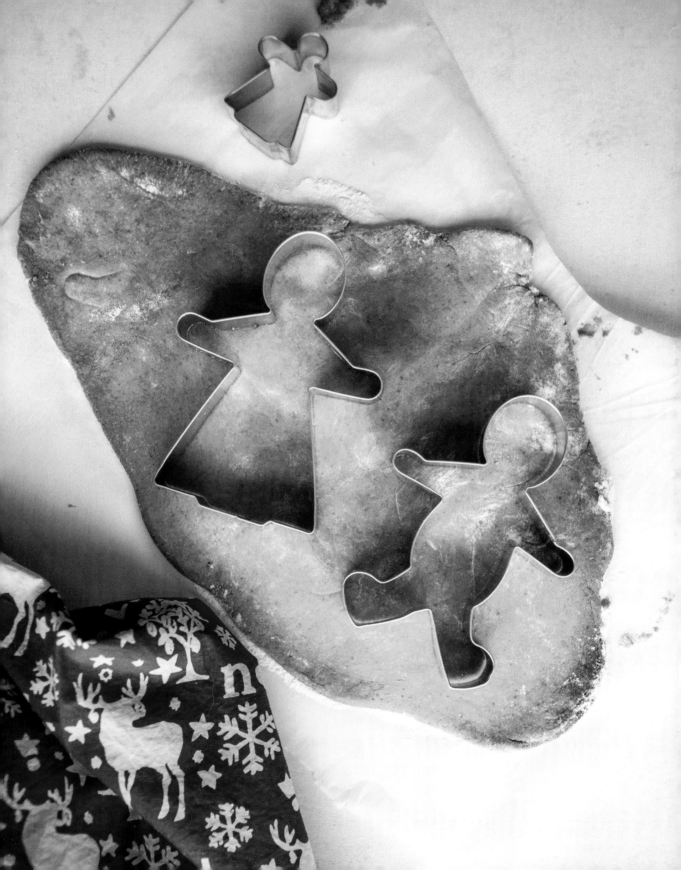

Christmas Crinkles

Yield: 24 cookies | Prep Time: 15 minutes | Cook Time: 12 minutes

You can turn out several batches of these in a hurry, so if you need a last-minute cookie to bring to your cookie exchange, this dessert is a snap to pull together.

INGREDIENTS

1 (15.25-ounce) box vanilla white cake mix

1 large egg

1 (8-ounce) container frozen whipped topping, thawed

1 teaspoon vanilla extract

Red and green food coloring

1 cup confectioners' sugar

DIRECTIONS

1. Preheat the oven to 350°F. Line a baking sheet with parchment paper.

2. In a large bowl, beat together the cake mix, egg, whipped topping, and vanilla.

3. Divide the dough in half and place one half in a second bowl. Add red food coloring to one bowl and green food coloring to the other. Add more food coloring to each as necessary until you reach the desired color.

4. Put the confectioners' sugar in a medium bowl. Using a cookie scoop, shape the dough into 2-inch balls and place into the bowl of confectioners' sugar. Roll around until covered. Place the balls on the baking sheet about 1 inch apart. Bake for 12 minutes, until set.

5. Cool for 5 minutes before serving.

So Easy Snowball Cookies

Yield: 24 cookies | Prep Time: 10–15 minutes | Cook Time: 10–12 minutes

While these cookies are a hit during the holiday season, I like to make them when I've started to hit the post-Christmas blues in the gray weeks in January and February. There's no better way to cheer up than with a freshly baked plate of cookies that brings you all the cheer of the holiday season.

INGREDIENTS

1 cup (2 sticks) unsalted butter, softened

½ cup confectioners' sugar, plus more for dusting

½ teaspoon salt

1 teaspoon almond extract

1 teaspoon vanilla extract

1½ cups all-purpose flour

½ cup cake flour

1½ cups finely ground almonds

DIRECTIONS

1. Preheat the oven to 350°F. Line two baking sheets with parchment paper.

2. In a large bowl, cream the butter and confectioners' sugar until light and fluffy. Add the salt, almond extract, vanilla extract, all-purpose flour, cake flour, and ground almonds and mix well. If the dough is too soft to handle, chill it for 20 to 30 minutes.

3. Using a cookie scoop, shape the dough into 1-inch balls and place them on the prepared baking sheets about 2 inches apart.

4. Bake for 10 to 12 minutes. Let the cookies cool.

5. Put a few tablespoons of confectioners' sugar in a bowl and roll the cookies in the sugar until fully coated. Place on a plate and serve.

Acknowledgments

My first week at gravitytank, maybe my second, I asked Kyleigh, my lead culinary designer, "What if something tastes bad?" I was very confused, coming from a world where your task was to make the best food you possibly could and into one where we made to fail and failed to learn. She looked at me with an expression that said, *That's the point.* She, like everyone, was there to help, to discuss, to brainstorm, and to learn, not to judge, criticize, or gossip. Thank you.

Kyleigh was just one of the wonderful people I met at gravitytank. Lucas, my boss, so to speak, changed my life. He taught me more than I ever thought I would know, cared so deeply about the work, and was by far one of the most intelligent minds I have ever met. Thank you.

To the rest of the gravitytank family, your ability to learn, to seek out knowledge and absorb it like a sponge, and to teach it to others, to find comfort in discovery, and to work hard every day to change our world is incredible. Thank you to Scott, Chris and Cira, Shailesh, Robert, Kariya, Susan, Dave, DVB, Justin, Sarah, Eleanor, Aaron, Ben, Tom, Maggee, Pooja, and Amaris. Thank you, everyone.

Thank you to my incredible culinary and creative team at Prime Publishing. Megan Von Schönhoff and Tom Krawczyk, my photographers. Chris Hammond, Judith Hines, and Marlene Stolfo, my culinary test-kitchen geniuses. To word masters Bryn Clark and Jessica Thelander. And to my amazing editor and friend, Kara Rota. Each book has been a team effort, filled with collaboration and creativity that reached no limits.

Index

Alex's Cowboy Cookies, 128, *129*
almonds, 10, *11*, 38, 39, *43*, 60, 61
    No-Bake Almond Coconut Cookies
        with, 67, 80, *81*
    Salted Caramel Bars with, 28, 29
    Snowball Cookies with, 220, *221*
Amish Sugar Cookies, Home-Style,
    98, 99
Andes mints, 144, 199
Apple Pie Bars, 3, *4*, 5

Bacon Peanut Butter Bars, *16*, 17
bananas, 6, 7
    Banana Bread Bites with, 67, 90, *91*
bar cookies
    Apple Pie Bars, 3, *4*, 5
    Better-Than-Anything Scotcharoos,
        40, 41
    Chocolate Chip Bars, 56, 57
    Chocolate Peanut Butter Bars,
        34, 35
    Dreamboat Caramel Bars, 32, 33
    Five-Layer Chocolate Cherry Bars,
        10, *11*
    Gooey Magic Cake Bars, *43*, 54, 55
    Gooey Turtle Bars, 124, *134*, 135
    Lemon Pie Bars, 52, 53
    No-Bake Coconut Graham Cracker
        Cookie Bars, 18, *19*
    Oatmeal Chocolate Raisin Bars,
        24, 25
    Orange Cream Bars, 70, *71*
    Peanut Butter Bacon Bars, *16*, 17
    Peanut Butter Bars, *12*, 13
    Peanut Butter Swirl Bars, 22, 23
    Pecan Pie Cheesecake Bars,
        168, 169
    Raspberry Oatmeal Cookie Bars,
        38, 39

Salted Caramel Bars, 28, 29
Seven Layers of Heaven, 8, 9
Spice Bars, *102*, 103
Stir and Bake Bars, 26, 27
Strawberry Bars, 74, *75*
Strawberry Cheesecake Bars,
    3, 14, *15*
Texas Gold Bars, 36, 37
3-Layer Nanaimo Bars, 6, 7
Trillionaire Dessert Bars, 3, 30, *31*
2-Ingredient Lemon Bars, 76, 77
Zebra Bars, 3, 20, 21
Best Chocolate Chip Cookies Ever,
    The, *126*, 127
Better-Than-Anything Scotcharoos,
    40, 41
Bite-Size Cinnamon Roll Cookies,
    97, 100, *101*
Blueberry Muffin Cookies, 94, 95
Breakfast Cookies, 182, *183*
Brownie Cookies, Buckeye, *125*,
    136, *137*
Brownie Cookies, Chewy, *132*, *133*
Butter Pecan Cake Mix Squares, 67,
    92, 93
Buttery Sugar Cookies, 104, *105*
Buttery Thumbprints, 120, *121*

cake mix recipes
    Chocolate Chip Bars, 56, 57
    Chocolate Cookies, *44*, 45
    Easy Oatmeal Cookies, 50, *51*
    Funfetti Cake Batter Cookies,
        43, *64*, 65
    Gooey Magic Cake Bars, *43*, 54, 55
    Lemon Pie Bars, 52, 53
    Magic Cream Cheese Squares, *43*,
        60, 61
    M&M's Drop Cookies, *43*, 58, 59

10-Minute Cool Whip Cookies,
    62, 63
10-Minute Miracle Cookies, 48, 49
Whipped Lemon Cookies, 46, *47*
caramel, 30, *31*, 32, 33, 156, *157*
    in Salted Caramel Bars, 28, 29
    in Salted Caramel Bites, 97,
        118, 119
    in Turtle Bars, 124, *134*, 135
    in Turtle Thumbprint Cookies,
        159, 174, *175*
cashews
    in Chocolate Haystacks, *125*, 130,
        131
    in No-Bake Cookie Clusters,
        68, 69
cheesecake bars
    Pecan Pie, *168*, 169
    Strawberry, 14, *15*
cherries, 182, *183*
    in Chocolate Cherry Blossom
        Cookies, 78, 79
    in Five-Layer Chocolate Cherry
        Bars, 10, *11*
Chewy Brownie Cookies, *132*, *133*
Chewy Classic Oatmeal Raisin
    Cookies, *172*, 173
Chewy Molasses Cookies, *176*, 177
chocolate-based recipes
    Alex's Cowboy Cookies, 128, *129*
    Best Chocolate Chip Cookies, The,
        126, 127
    Caramel Macchiato Cookies, 156,
        157
    Chewy Brownie Cookies, *132*, *133*
    Chocolate Chip Cookies 'n' Cream,
        154, 155
    Chocolate Haystacks, *125*, *130*, 131
    Chocolate Shortbread, *125*, *146*,
        147

chocolate-based recipes (continued)
  Cream Cheese Chocolate Chip
    Cookies, 140, 141
  5-Minute No-Bake Cookies,
    138, 139
  Gooey Turtle Bars, 124, 134, 135
  Incredible Buckeye Brownie
    Cookies, 125, 136, 137
  Mint Chocolate Cookies, 124, 125,
    144, 145
  Mocha Polka Dot Cookies, 152, 153
  Monster Cookies, 142, 143
  My-Goodness-These-Are-Amazing
    Cookies, 150, 151
  Toasted S'mores Cookies, 148, 149
chocolate as ingredient in
  Banana Bread Bites, 67, 90, 91
  Better-Than-Anything Scotcharoos,
    40, 41
  Breakfast Cookies, 182, 183
  Brownie Cookies, Chewy, 132, 133
  Caramel Bars, Dreamboat, 32, 33
  Chocolate Cake Mix Cookies,
    44, 45
  Chocolate Cherry Blossom
    Cookies, 78, 79
  Chocolate Chip Bars, 56, 57
  Chocolate Kiss Surprise Powder
    Puff Cookies, 210, 211
  Chocolate Peanut Butter Bars,
    34, 35
  Christmas Magic Squares, 193,
    196, 197
  Five-Layer Chocolate Cherry Bars,
    10, 11
  glaze, 30, 31, 160, 161, 166, 167
  No-Bake Almond Coconut
    Cookies, 67, 80, 81
  Oatmeal Chocolate Chip Cookies,
    Homemade, 164, 165
  Oatmeal Chocolate Raisin Bars,
    24, 25
  Oatmeal Cookies, Easy, 50, 51
  Peanut Butter Bacon Bars, 16, 17
  Peanut Butter Swirl Bars, 22, 23
  Salted Caramel Bars, 28, 29
  Seven Layers of Heaven, 8, 9

Stained Glass Window Cookies,
  208, 209
Stir and Bake Bars, 26, 27
Thumbprint Cookies, Red Velvet,
  184, 185, 203
Thumbprint Cookies, Turtle, 159,
  174, 175
topping, 6, 7, 160, 161
Trillionaire Dessert Bars, 30, 31
Zebra Bars, 3, 20, 21
Christmas Crinkles, 218, 219
Christmas Magic Squares, 193,
  196, 197
cinnamon, 3, 4, 5, 24, 25, 38, 39, 67,
  74, 75, 90, 91, 97, 120, 121, 162,
  163, 164, 165, 172, 173, 182, 183
  candy, in Jolly Holly Cookies,
    202, 203
  in Cinnamon Roll Cookies, Bite-
    Size, 97, 100, 101
  in Ginger Snaps, 97, 108, 109
  in Molasses Cookies, Chewy, 176,
    177
  in Snickerdoodles, 106, 107
  in Spice Bars, 102, 103
  in Spice Cookies, Danish, 97,
    112, 113
  in Spice Cookies, Grandma's,
    122, 123
Classic French Madeleines, 159,
  178, 179
coconut, 8, 9, 10, 11, 26, 27, 128, 129,
  193, 196, 197, 208, 209
  in Gooey Magic Cake Bars, 43,
    54, 55
  in Lemon Coconut Cookies, 82, 83
  in Nana's Best Coconut Macaroons,
    170, 171
  in No-Bake Almond Coconut
    Cookies, 67, 80, 81
  in No-Bake Coconut Graham
    Cracker Cookie Bars, 18, 19
  in Tropical Paradise Cookies, 67,
    84, 85
cookie(s). See also specific categories
  bars, 2–41, 3–4, 7–8, 11–12, 15–16,
    19–20, 23–24, 27–28, 31–32,

35–36, 39–40, 43, 52, 53, 54, 55,
  56, 57, 70, 71, 74, 75–76, 77, 102,
  103, 124, 134, 135, 168, 169, 204,
  205
  cake-mix, 42–65, 43–44, 47–48,
    51–52, 55–56, 59–60, 63–64
  chocolate-based, 124–56, 125–26,
    129–30, 133–34, 137–38, 141–42,
    145–46, 149–50, 153–54, 157
  fruit- and nut-based, 66–94, 67–68,
    71–72, 75–76, 79–80, 83–84,
    87–88, 91–92, 95
  holiday, 192–220, 193–94, 197–98,
    201–2, 205–6, 209–10, 213–14,
    217–18, 221
  old-fashioned, 158–90, 159–60,
    163–64, 167–68, 171–72, 175–76,
    179–80, 183–84, 187–88, 191
  organization/pre-planning for, 1
  sugar and spice, 96–132, 97–98,
    101–2, 105–6, 109–10, 113–14,
    117–18, 121–22, 133
Cool Whip Cookies, 10-Minute,
  62, 63
cranberries, 172, 173
  Cranberry Orange Cookies with,
    88, 89
  White Chocolate Cranberry
    Cookies with, 214, 215
cream cheese, 70, 71, 184, 185
  Cake Mix Magic Cream Cheese
    Squares with, 43, 60, 61
  Cream Cheese Chocolate Chip
    Cookies with, 140, 141
  Cream Cheese Strawberry Cookies
    with, 86, 87

Danish Spice Cookies, 97, 112, 113
Dreamboat Caramel Bars, 32, 33

Easy Oatmeal Cookies, 50, 51
Easy Pecan Pie Bars, 204, 205
espresso, 45, 136, 139
  in Caramel Macchiato Cookies,
    156, 157

in chocolate glaze, *160, 161*
in Mocha Polka Dot Cookies, *152, 153*

Fancy Flours, 112
Fante's Kitchen Shop, 112
Five-Layer Chocolate Cherry Bars, *10, 11*
5-Minute No-Bake Cookies, *138, 139*
frosting. *See also* glaze
   for cinnamon rolls, 97, 100, *101*
   cream cheese, 70, *71*
   for Italian Christmas Cookies, *193, 206, 207*
   soda pop, *110, 111*
fruit and nut recipes. *See also* nuts
   Banana Bread Bites, 67, 90, *91*
   Blueberry Muffin Cookies, 94, 95
   Butter Pecan Cake Mix Squares, 67, 92, 93
   Chocolate Cherry Blossom Cookies, 78, 79
   Crazy Good Cranberry Orange Cookies, 88, 89
   Cream Cheese Strawberry Cookies, 86, 87
   Lemon Coconut Cookies, 82, 83
   No-Bake Almond Coconut Cookies, 67, 80, 81
   No-Bake Cookie Clusters, 68, 69
   Orange Cream Bars, 70, *71*
   Pecan Sandies, 72, 73
   Strawberry Bars, 74, 75
   Tropical Paradise Cookies, 67, *84, 85*
   2-Ingredient Lemon Bars, 76, 77
fruits, 120, *121*
   apple, 3, *4, 5*
   banana, 6, *7*, 67, 90, *91*
   blueberries, 94, 95
   coconut, 8, 9, 18, *19, 43, 54, 55*, 67, 80, 81, 82, 83, *84, 85*, 128, *129, 170, 171, 193, 196, 197, 208, 209*
   cranberry, 88, 89, *172, 173, 214, 215*
   lemon, 46, *47*, 52, 53, 76, 77, 82, 83, 200, *201*

orange, 70, *71*, 88, 89
pineapple, 67, *84, 85, 193, 206, 207*
raspberry, 38, 39, *114, 115*
strawberry, *14, 15*, 74, 75, 86, 87
Funfetti Cake Batter Cookies, *43, 64, 65*

ginger
   in Danish Spice Cookies, 97, 112, *113*
   in Gingerbread People, 216, 217
   in Ginger Snaps, 97, 108, *109*
   in Molasses Cookies, Chewy, *176, 177*
   in Spice Cookies, Grandma's, *122, 123*
glaze, 94, 95, *188, 189, 193, 206, 207.* *See also* frosting
   chocolate, 30, *31, 166, 167*
   chocolate-espresso, *160, 161*
   maple, 116, *117*
Gooey Magic Cake Bars, *43, 54, 55*
Gooey Turtle Bars, 124, *134, 135*
Grandma's Spice Cookies, *122, 123*

Half-Moon Cookies, *159, 166, 167*
hazelnuts, 67, 80, 81, 88, 89
   in 5-Minute No-Bake Cookies, *138, 139*
   in My-Goodness-These-Are-Amazing Cookies, *150, 151*
holiday recipes
   Chocolate Kiss Surprise Powder Puff Cookies, 210, 211
   Christmas Crinkles, *218, 219*
   Christmas Magic Squares, *193, 196, 197*
   Easy Pecan Pie Bars, 204, 205
   Gingerbread People, 216, 217
   Italian Christmas Cookies, *193, 206, 207*
   Jolly Holly Cookies, 202, 203
   North Pole Lemon Cookies, 200, 201

Peppermint Crunch Balls, *193, 198, 199*
Pizzelles, *193, 212, 213*
So Easy Snowball Cookies, 220, 221
Stained Glass Window Cookies, 208, 209
3-Ingredient Pumpkin Cake Cookies, *194, 195*
Unforgettable White Chocolate Cranberry Cookies, *214, 215*
Homemade Oatmeal Chocolate Chip Cookies, *164, 165*
Home-Style Amish Sugar Cookies, 98, 99

Incredible Buckeye Brownie Cookies, *125, 136, 137*
Italian Almond Balls. *See* Russian Tea Cakes
Italian Christmas Cookies, *193, 206, 207*

Jolly Holly Cookies, 202, 203

Lemon Bars, 2-Ingredient, 76, 77
Lemon Coconut Cookies, 82, 83
Lemon Cookies, North Pole, 200, *201*
Lemon Pie Bars, 52, 53
Linzer Cookies, *114, 115*

macadamia nuts, *214, 215*
   in Gooey Magic Cake Bars, *43, 54, 55*
   in Tropical Paradise Cookies, 67, *84, 85*
Macaroons, Nana's Best Coconut, 170, *171*
macerating process, 86
Madeleines, Classic French, *159, 178, 179*
Magic Cream Cheese Squares, Cake Mix, *43, 60, 61*

Magic Gooey Cake Bars, *43*, 54, 55
Maple Sugar Cookies, 116, *117*
marshmallows
    in Jolly Holly Cookies, 202, 203
    in No-Bake Cookie Clusters, 68, 69
    in Stained Glass Window Cookies, 208, *209*
    in Toasted S'mores Cookies, 148, *149*
Mexican Wedding Cookies. *See* Russian Tea Cakes
mint(s)
    Andes, 144, 199
    Mint Chocolate Cookies with, 124, *125*, 144, *145*
    Peppermint Crunch Balls with, *193*, 198, 199
Miracle Cookies, 10-Minute, *48*, 49
M&M's
    Drop Cookies, *43*, 58, 59
    in Monster Cookies, *142*, 143
Mocha Polka Dot Cookies, 152, *153*
molasses
    in Chewy Molasses Cookies, *176*, 177
    in Gingerbread People, 216, *217*
    in Ginger Snaps, 97, 108, *109*
    in Grandma's Spice Cookies, *122*, 123
Monster Cookies, *142*, 143
Muffin Cookies, Blueberry, 94, 95
My-Goodness-These-Are-Amazing Cookies, 150, 151

Nana's Best Coconut Macaroons, 170, *171*
No-Bake Almond Coconut Cookies, *67*, 80, 81
No-Bake Coconut Graham Cracker Cookie Bars, 18, *19*
No-Bake Cookie Clusters, 68, 69
No-Bake 5-Minute Cookies, 138, 139
No-Bake Peanut Butter Pretzel Bites, *159*, 160, 161
North Pole Lemon Cookies, 200, *201*

nuts. *See also* fruit and nut recipes; *specific nuts*
    almonds, 10, *11*, 28, 29, 38, 39, *43*, 60, 61, *67*, 80, 81, 220, *221*
    cashews, 68, 69, *125*, 130, 131
    hazelnut, *67*, 80, 81, 88, 89, *138*, 139, *150*, 151
    macadamia, *43*, 54, 55, *67*, 84, 85, *214*, 215
    peanut butter, 12, 13, 16, 17, 22, 23, 32, 33, 34, 35, 40, 41, 68, 69, *125*, 130, 131, 136, *137*, *138*, 139, *142*, 143, *150*, 151, *159*, 160, 161, 182, 183, 190, *191*
    pecans, 3, 6, 7, 8, 9, 20, 21, *67*, 72, 73, 90, *91*, 92, 93, *102*, 103, 124, 128, *129*, 134, 135, *159*, 162, *163*, *164*, 165, 168, 169, 172, 173, *174*, *175*, 186, *187*, 204, 205
    walnuts, 3, 4, 5, 18, *19*, 26, 27, *43*, 50, *51*, 56, 57, 60, 61, 132, *133*, 182, 183, *193*, 196, 197, 208, 209

oatmeal recipes
    Oatmeal Chocolate Chip Cookies, Homemade, *164*, 165
    Oatmeal Chocolate Raisin Bars, *24*, 25
    Oatmeal Cookies, Easy, 50, *51*
    Oatmeal Raisin Cookies, Classic, *172*, 173
    Oatmeal Raspberry Cookie Bars, 38, 39
old-fashioned recipes
    Breakfast Cookies, 182, 183
    Chewy Classic Oatmeal Raisin Cookies, *172*, 173
    Chewy Molasses Cookies, *176*, 177
    Classic French Madeleines, *159*, 178, *179*
    Half-Moon Cookies, *159*, 166, *167*
    Homemade Oatmeal Chocolate Chip Cookies, *164*, 165
    Nana's Best Coconut Macaroons, 170, *171*

Peanut Butter Pretzel Bites, *159*, 160, 161
Pecan Pie Cheesecake Bars, 168, 169
Red Velvet Thumbprints, *184*, 185, 203
Ricotta Cookies, *188*, 189
Russian Tea Cakes, 162, *163*
Soft Peanut Butter Cookies, 190, *191*
3-Ingredient Old-Fashioned Shortbread Buttons, *180*, 181
Toffee Butter Icebox Cookies, 186, *187*
Turtle Thumbprint Cookies, *159*, 174, *175*
Orange Cranberry Cookies, Crazy Good, 88, 89
Orange Cream Bars, 70, *71*
orange juice, macerating with, 86

peanut butter, 32, 33, *40*, 41, 68, 69, *125*, 130, 131, 136, *137*, *138*, 139, *142*, 143, *150*, 151, 182, 183
    Chocolate Peanut Butter Bars with, 34, 35
    Peanut Butter Bacon Bars with, 16, 17
    Peanut Butter Bars with, *12*, 13
    Peanut Butter Cookies, Soft, with, 190, *191*
    Peanut Butter Pretzel Bites with, *159*, 160, 161
    Peanut Butter Swirl Bars with, 22, 23
pecans, 3, 6, 7, 8, 9, 20, 21, *67*, 90, *91*, 102, 103, 124, 128, *129*, 134, 135, *159*, 162, *163*, *164*, 165, 172, 173, *174*, *175*, 186, *187*
    Butter Pecan Cake Mix Squares with, *67*, 92, 93
    Pecan Pie Bars, Easy, with, 204, 205
    Pecan Pie Cheesecake Bars with, 168, 169
    Pecan Sandies with, 72, 73

Peppermint Crunch Balls, *193*, *198*, 199

Pillsbury Moist Supreme Cake Mix, 14, *15*

pineapple
  in Italian Christmas Cookies, *193*, 206, 207
  in Tropical Paradise Cookies, 67, 84, 85

Pizzelles, *193*, 212, *213*

Pretzel Bites, Peanut Butter, *159*, *160*, 161

Pumpkin Cake Cookies, 3-Ingredient, *194*, 195

raisins, *102*, 103, 128, *129*
  Oatmeal Chocolate Raisin Bars with, 24, 25
  Oatmeal Raisin Cookies, Classic, with, *172*, 173

raspberries, *114*, 115
  Raspberry Oatmeal Cookie Bars with, 38, 39

Red Velvet Thumbprints, *184*, 185, 203

Ricotta Cookies, *188*, 189

Russian Tea Cakes, *162*, 163

Salted Caramel Bars, 28, 29

Salted Caramel Bites, *97*, *118*, 119

Seven Layers of Heaven, 8, 9

Shortbread Buttons, 3-Ingredient, *180*, 181

Shortbread, Chocolate, *125*, *146*, 147

S'mores Cookies, Toasted, 148, *149*

Snickerdoodles, *106*, 107

Soda Pop Cookies, *110*, 111

So Easy Snowball Cookies, 220, *221*

Soft Peanut Butter Cookies, 190, *191*

Special K Oats & Honey cereal, *150*, 151

speculoos. See Danish Spice Cookies

Spice Bars, *102*, 103

sprinkles, *40*, 41, 62, *63*, 98, 99, 104, *105*, *142*, 143, *193*, 206, 207
  Funfetti Cake Batter Cookies with, *43*, *64*, 65

Stained Glass Window Cookies, 208, 209

Stir and Bake Bars, 26, 27

strawberries
  Cream Cheese Strawberry Cookies with, 86, 87
  Strawberry Bars with, 74, 75
  Strawberry Cheesecake Bars with, 3, 14, *15*

sugar and spice recipes
  Bite-Size Cinnamon Roll Cookies, *97*, 100, *101*
  Buttery Sugar Cookies, 104, *105*
  Buttery Thumbprints, 120, *121*
  Danish Spice Cookies, *97*, 112, *113*
  Ginger Snaps, *97*, 108, *109*
  Grandma's Spice Cookies, *122*, 123
  Home-Style Amish Sugar Cookies, 98, 99
  Linzer Cookies, *114*, 115
  Maple Sugar Cookies, 116, *117*
  Salted Caramel Bites, *97*, *118*, 119
  Snickerdoodles, *106*, 107
  Soda Pop Cookies, *110*, 111
  Spice Bars, *102*, 103

sugar cookies
  Buttery, 104, *105*
  Home-Style Amish, 98, 99
  Maple, 116, *117*

10-Minute Cool Whip Cookies, 62, *63*

10-Minute Miracle Cookies, 48, 49

Texas Gold Bars, 36, 37

3-Ingredient Old-Fashioned Shortbread Buttons, *180*, 181

3-Ingredient Pumpkin Cake Cookies, *194*, 195

3-Layer Nanaimo Bars, 6, 7

thumbprint cookies
  Buttery, 120, *121*
  Red Velvet, *184*, 185, 203
  Turtle, *159*, *174*, *175*

Toasted S'mores Cookies, 148, *149*

toffee, 8, 9, *40*, 41, *193*, 196, *197*
  in Toffee Butter Icebox Cookies, *186*, 187

Trillionaire Dessert Bars, 3, 30, *31*

Tropical Paradise Cookies, 67, 84, 85

Turtle Bars, Gooey, *124*, *134*, 135

Turtle Thumbprint Cookies, *159*, *174*, *175*

2-Ingredient Lemon Bars, 76, 77

Unforgettable White Chocolate Cranberry Cookies, *214*, 215

walnuts, 3, *4*, 5, 50, *51*, 56, 57
  in Breakfast Cookies, *182*, 183
  in Brownie Cookies, 132, *133*
  in Christmas Magic Squares, *193*, 196, *197*
  in Magic Cream Cheese Squares, *43*, 60, 61
  in No-Bake Coconut Graham Cracker Cookie Bars, 18, *19*
  in Stained Glass Window Cookies, 208, 209
  in Stir and Bake Bars, 26, 27

Whipped Lemon Cookies, 46, 47

White Chocolate Cranberry Cookies, *214*, 215

Zebra Bars, 3, 20, 21

About the Author

After receiving her master's in culinary arts at Auguste Escoffier in Avignon, France, Addie stayed in France to learn from Christian Etienne at his three-Michelin-star restaurant. Upon leaving France, she spent the next several years working with restaurant groups. She worked in the kitchen for Daniel Boulud and moved coast to coast with Thomas Keller building a career in management, restaurant openings, and brand development. She later joined Martha Stewart Living Omnimedia, where she worked with the editorial team as well as in marketing and sales. While living in New York, Addie completed her bachelor's degree in organizational behavior. Upon leaving New York, Addie joined gravitytank, an innovation consultancy in Chicago. As a culinary designer at gravitytank, Addie designed new food products for companies large and small. She created edible prototypes for clients and research participants to taste and experience, some of which you may see in stores today. In 2015, she debuted on the Food Network, where she competed on *Cutthroat Kitchen* and won!

Addie is the executive producer for RecipeLion. She oversees and creates culinary content for multiple web platforms and communities, leads video strategy, and manages the production of in-print books. Addie is passionate about taking easy recipes and making them elegant, from fine dining and entertaining to innovation and test kitchens. She calls this Easy Elegant Entertaining.

Addie and her husband live in Lake Forest, Illinois, with their happy puppy, Paisley. Addie is actively involved with youth culinary programs in the Chicagoland area and serves on the board of a bakery and catering company that employs at-risk youth. She is a healthy-food teacher for first graders in a low-income school district, and aside from eating and entertaining with friends and family, she loves encouraging kids to be creative in the kitchen!

Addie makes dinner every night. It's never perfect, sometimes delicious, and always fun.